EveryDay Is Christmas
A
365-Day Prayer Book

Written by

Betty J. Christmas

This Prayer Book Belongs To

_____

"Always be joyful. Never stop praying. Be thankful in all circumstances, for this is God's will for you who belong to Christ Jesus."

1 Thessalonians 5:16-18 NLT

Dear Beloved Reader,

As you embark on this year-long journey of prayer through "EveryDay is Christmas," I want to take a moment to remind you of the incredible power that prayer holds. In a world filled with challenges and uncertainties, prayer is your steadfast anchor, a lifeline that connects you to the heart of God.

I encourage you to be steadfast in your commitment to prayer. Each day is a precious opportunity to communicate with the Creator, to seek His guidance, and to express your heart's desires.

Remember, prayer is not merely about asking; it is about building a relationship—a relationship that deepens as you pour out your soul before Him and listen for His voice.

As you immerse yourself in these prayers, may you find strength, comfort, and hope. Let each prayer serve as a reminder of God's unwavering love and faithfulness. Trust that He hears every word and sees every tear. Your prayers have the power to transform your life and the lives of those around you.

Be persistent. Be expectant. God is always at work, even when you cannot see it. Embrace this journey with an open heart and a willing spirit, and watch as God unfolds His beautiful plans in your life.

Stay committed to prayer, and let it be the foundation upon which you build your faith. I am praying for you and believe that this year will be a season of divine encounters and answered prayers.

In His love and grace,

Apostle BJ Christmas

Table Of Contents

Introduction: The Power of Prayer   1

Why We Should Pray   1

The Importance of Prayer for a Believer   2

Prayer 1: God's Unfailing Love   3

Prayer 2: The God Who Sees Me   4

Prayer 3: Rest for the Weary   5

Prayer 4: Strength in Times of Trouble   6

Prayer 5: God's Grace in My Weakness   7

Prayer 6: The Light of the World   8

Prayer 7: God's Faithfulness to Keep His Promises   9

Prayer 8: Trusting God's Timing   10

Prayer 9: Peace in the Storm   11

Prayer 10: God's Guidance in Every Decision   12

Prayer 11: God, My Ever-Present Help   13

Prayer 12: Trusting in God's Faithfulness   14

Prayer 13: Peace Beyond Understanding   15

Prayer 14: Renew My Strength, Lord   16

Prayer 15: God's Plans Are Perfect   17

Prayer 16: God, My Shield and Defender   18

Prayer 17: Confidence in God's Timing   19

Prayer 18: Walking by Faith   20

Prayer 19: God's Unshakable Word   21

Prayer 20: God's Light in My Darkness   22

Prayer 21: Strength in My Weakness   23

Prayer 22: Living in God's Freedom   24

Prayer 23: God, My Refuge and Strength   25

Prayer 24: God's Grace to Forgive 26

Prayer 25: Trusting in God's Faithfulness 27

Prayer 26: God's Healing Touch 28

Prayer 27: Walking in God's Wisdom 29

Prayer 28: God's Promise of Peace 30

Prayer 29: God's Mercy Endures Forever 31

Prayer 30: God's Power at Work in Me 32

Prayer 31: The Lord Is My Shepherd 33

Prayer 32: Walking in Love 34

Prayer 33: God's Strength in the Battle 35

Prayer 34: God's Peace in the Waiting 36

Prayer 35: Guarding My Heart 37

Prayer 36: God's Compassion for the Weary 38

Prayer 37: Embracing God's Grace 39

Prayer 38: Walking in Righteousness 40

Prayer 39: Trusting God in the Unknown 41

Prayer 40: God's Everlasting Covenant 42

Prayer 41: God's Light That Shines in the Darkness 43

Prayer 42: God's Wisdom in Every Decision 44

Prayer 43: Trusting in God's Protection 45

Prayer 44: God's Joy is My Strength 46

Prayer 45: Trusting God to Provide 47

Prayer 46: God's Grace is Sufficient 48

Prayer 47: God's Word Brings Life 49

Prayer 48: Peace in the Midst of the Storm 50

Prayer 49: God's Strength to Overcome Temptation 51

Prayer 50: Restoring My Soul 52

Prayer 51: God's Light in My Darkness 53

Prayer 52: The Lord Is My Salvation 54

Prayer 53: God's Peace to Guard My Heart 55

Prayer 54: God's Help in My Time of Need 56

Prayer 55: New Heart and Spirit 57

Prayer 56: God's Strength in My Weakness 58

Prayer 57: God's Faithfulness Through Every Season 59

Prayer 58: God's Healing Power 60

Prayer 59: Renewing My Mind in Christ 61

Prayer 60: God's Strength in Spiritual Battles 62

Prayer 61: God's Promise to Answer My Prayers 63

Prayer 62: Walking in God's Light 64

Prayer 63: God's Unfailing Love 65

Prayer 64: God's Strength in Trials 66

Prayer 65: Trusting in God's Goodness 67

Prayer 66: God's Faithfulness in Answering Prayers 68

Prayer 67: God's Compassion and Grace 69

Prayer 68: Walking in the Light of God 70

Prayer 69: God's Power to Deliver 71

Prayer 70: God's Faithfulness to Fulfill His Promises 72

Prayer 71: Trusting God's Plans for My Life 73

Prayer 72: God's Comfort in Times of Sorrow 74

Prayer 73: God's Wisdom in Every Situation 75

Prayer 74: God's Provision in Every Season 76

Prayer 75: God's Protection Over My Life 77

Prayer 76: God's Peace in My Heart 78

Prayer 77: God's Compassion Toward Me 79

Prayer 78: Strength in Times of Waiting 80

Prayer 79: God's Guidance in My Life 81

Prayer 80: Walking in God's Love 82

Prayer 81: Trusting God's Promise of Protection 83

Prayer 82: God's Unfailing Word 84

Prayer 83: God's Power in My Life 85

Prayer 84: God's Mercy in My Life   86

Prayer 85: God's Everlasting Covenant   87

Prayer 86: God's Guidance in Every Step   88

Prayer 87: God's Peace in My Soul   89

Prayer 88: God's Abundant Grace   90

Prayer 89: God's Faithfulness in My Journey   91

Prayer 90: The Blessing of Obedience   92

Prayer 91: God's Presence in My Life   93

Prayer 92: God's Healing in My Life   94

Prayer 93: God's Strength in My Faith   95

Prayer 94: God's Love in My Relationships   96

Prayer 95: God's Light Guiding My Way   97

Prayer 96: God's Joy in My Life   98

Prayer 97: God's Faithfulness Through Trials   99

Prayer 98: God's Comfort in Times of Need   100

Prayer 99: God's Promise of New Beginnings   101

Prayer 100: God's Light in the Darkness   102

Prayer 101: God's Presence in My Life   103

Prayer 102: God's Wisdom in My Choices   104

Prayer 103: God's Faithfulness in My Life   105

Prayer 104: God's Compassion for the Brokenhearted   106

Prayer 105: God's Peace Amidst Chaos   107

Prayer 106: God's Comfort in Trials   108

Prayer 107: God's Promise of Restoration   109

Prayer 108: God's Love is Unconditional   110

Prayer 109: God's Faithfulness in All Things   111

Prayer 110: God's Strength in My Journey   112

Prayer 111: God's Guidance Through the Unknown   113

Prayer 112: God's Promise of Hope   114

Prayer 113: God's Peace in the Storm   115

Prayer 114: God's Restoration in My Life   116

Prayer 115: God's Comfort in Grief   117

Prayer 116: God's Strength in My Journey   118

Prayer 117: God's Wisdom for the Future   119

Prayer 118: God's Healing for My Soul   120

Prayer 119: God's Faithfulness in Every Trial   121

Prayer 120: God's Blessing Over My Life   122

Prayer 121: God's Assurance of His Presence   123

Prayer 122: God's Perfect Timing   124

Prayer 123: God's Compassionate Heart   125

Prayer 124: God's Wisdom in the Trials   126

Prayer 125: God's Comfort in My Grief   127

Prayer 126: God's Promise of Restoration   128

Prayer 127: God's Faithfulness Through Trials   129

Prayer 128: God's Light in My Life   130

Prayer 129: God's Love is Unconditional   131

Prayer 130: God's Strength in My Weakness   132

Prayer 131: God's Peace in Times of Trouble   133

Prayer 132: God's Faithfulness in Every Season   134

Prayer 133: God's Goodness in My Life   135

Prayer 134: God's Call to Love Others   136

Prayer 135: God's Strength in My Challenges   137

Prayer 136: God's Promise of Hope and Healing   138

Prayer 137: God's Comfort in the Storm   139

Prayer 138: God's Goodness and Mercy   140

Prayer 139: God's Faithfulness Through Trials   141

Prayer 140: God's Promise of Peace   142

Prayer 141: God's Abundant Provision   143

Prayer 142: God's Hope in My Life   144

Prayer 143: God's Light in My Darkness   145

Prayer 144: God's Rest for My Soul 146

Prayer 145: God's Deliverance from Fear 147

Prayer 146: God's Joy in My Life 148

Prayer 147: God's Purpose in My Life 149

Prayer 148: God's Assurance of His Love 150

Prayer 149: God's Wisdom in My Decisions 151

Prayer 150: God's Grace in My Weakness 152

Prayer 151: God's Promises of Restoration 153

Prayer 152: God's Faithfulness in Every Circumstance 154

Prayer 153: God's Goodness in My Life 155

Prayer 154: God's Assurance in Times of Trouble 156

Prayer 155: God's Encouragement in the Journey 157

Prayer 156: God's Joy in My Heart 158

Prayer 157: God's Promises in My Life 159

Prayer 158: God's Hope in Every Situation 160

Prayer 159: God's Love is Unchanging 161

Prayer 160: God's Strength in My Weakness 162

Prayer 161: God's Comfort in Sorrow 163

Prayer 162: God's Faithfulness in Every Season 164

Prayer 163: God's Abundant Mercy 165

Prayer 164: God's Strength in Trials 166

Prayer 165: God's Promise of Restoration 167

Prayer 166: God's Faithfulness in Every Challenge 168

Prayer 167: God's Light in the Darkness 169

Prayer 168: God's Abiding Presence 170

Prayer 169: God's Goodness in My Life 171

Prayer 170: God's Promise of Healing 172

Prayer 171: God's Grace in My Weakness 173

Prayer 172: God's Promise of Peace 174

Prayer 173: God's Power in My Life 175

Prayer 174: God's Faithfulness in Difficult Times   176

Prayer 175: God's Protection Over My Life   177

Prayer 176: God's Provision in Every Need   178

Prayer 177: God's Comfort in My Pain   179

Prayer 178: God's Wisdom in Every Decision   180

Prayer 179: God's Strength in My Weakness   181

Prayer 180: God's Goodness in All Things   182

Prayer 181: God's Peace in Troubling Times   183

Prayer 182: God's Faithfulness Through Every Season   184

Prayer 183: God's Restoration in My Life   185

Prayer 184: God's Love is Unchanging   186

Prayer 185: God's Wisdom in My Decisions   187

Prayer 186: God's Protection Over My Life   188

Prayer 187: God's Faithfulness in My Life   189

Prayer 188: God's Goodness in Every Situation   190

Prayer 189: God's Hope in My Heart   191

Prayer 190: God's Strength in My Journey   192

Prayer 191: God's Assurance in Trials   193

Prayer 192: God's Goodness in All Things   194

Prayer 193: God's Comfort in Grief   195

Prayer 194: God's Guidance in My Life   196

Prayer 195: God's Restoration in My Life   197

Prayer 196: God's Faithfulness Through Every Season   198

Prayer 197: God's Joy in My Heart   199

Prayer 198: God's Promises of Hope   200

Prayer 199: God's Abundant Grace   201

Prayer 200: God's Love is Everlasting   202

Prayer 201: God's Presence in Times of Trouble   203

Prayer 202: God's Hope for the Future   204

Prayer 203: God's Strength in My Trials   205

Prayer 204: God's Love for Me   206

Prayer 205: God's Comfort in Sorrow   207

Prayer 206: God's Guidance in My Life   208

Prayer 207: God's Mercy and Grace   209

Prayer 208: God's Protection Over My Heart   210

Prayer 209: God's Joy in Every Season   211

Prayer 210: God's Assurance of His Love   212

Prayer 211: God's Strength in My Trials   213

Prayer 212: God's Presence in Difficult Times   214

Prayer 213: God's Assurance of His Love   215

Prayer 214: God's Healing Touch   216

Prayer 215: God's Comfort in Sorrow   217

Prayer 216: God's Guidance in Every Step   218

Prayer 217: God's Joy in My Life   219

Prayer 218: God's Peace in Every Storm   220

Prayer 219: God's Faithfulness Through All Seasons   221

Prayer 220: God's Purpose in My Life   222

Prayer 221: God's Healing Power   223

Prayer 222: God's Strength in Weakness   224

Prayer 223: God's Love Endures Forever   225

Prayer 224: God's Peace in the Midst of Chaos   226

Prayer 225: God's Promise of Restoration   227

Prayer 226: God's Faithfulness in Every Trial   228

Prayer 227: God's Abundant Grace   229

Prayer 228: God's Guidance in Every Decision   230

Prayer 229: God's Love is Everlasting   231

Prayer 230: God's Assurance in Difficult Times   232

Prayer 231: God's Hope in My Heart   233

Prayer 232: God's Abundant Provision   234

Prayer 233: God's Faithfulness in My Life   235

Prayer 234: God's Joy in My Journey 236

Prayer 235: God's Comfort in My Life 237

Prayer 236: God's Light in My Life 238

Prayer 237: God's Assurance of His Presence 239

Prayer 238: God's Purpose for My Life 240

Prayer 239: God's Love in My Relationships 241

Prayer 240: God's Assurance in Uncertainty 242

Prayer 241: God's Healing in My Life 243

Prayer 242: God's Strength in Adversity 244

Prayer 243: God's Joy in My Heart 245

Prayer 244: God's Peace in My Life 246

Prayer 245: God's Faithfulness Through Trials 247

Prayer 246: God's Provision for My Needs 248

Prayer 247: God's Assurance in My Life 249

Prayer 248: God's Mercy in My Life 250

Prayer 249: God's Light in My Darkness 251

Prayer 250: God's Assurance in All Circumstances 252

Prayer 251: God's Promise of Restoration 253

Prayer 252: God's Strength in Every Season 254

Prayer 253: God's Faithfulness in All Things 255

Prayer 254: God's Comfort in Times of Grief 256

Prayer 255: God's Peace in My Heart 257

Prayer 256: God's Goodness in My Life 258

Prayer 257: God's Light in My Darkness 259

Prayer 258: God's Guidance in My Life 260

Prayer 259: God's Faithfulness in Every Situation 261

Prayer 260: God's Hope for the Future 262

Prayer 261: God's Peace in Troubling Times 263

Prayer 262: God's Faithfulness in Every Challenge 264

Prayer 263: God's Comfort in My Weakness 265

Prayer 264: God's Joy in My Life   266

Prayer 265: God's Provision in My Life   267

Prayer 266: God's Assurance of His Love   268

Prayer 267: God's Light in My Life   269

Prayer 268: God's Comfort in Times of Sorrow   270

Prayer 269: God's Wisdom in My Decisions   271

Prayer 270: God's Hope for the Future   272

Prayer 271: God's Assurance in Difficult Times   273

Prayer 272: God's Healing Presence   274

Prayer 273: God's Light in Darkness   275

Prayer 274: God's Faithfulness in Every Season   276

Prayer 275: God's Love in My Life   277

Prayer 276: God's Purpose in My Journey   278

Prayer 277: God's Strength in My Weakness   279

Prayer 278: God's Hope in Troubling Times   280

Prayer 279: God's Assurance of His Presence   281

Prayer 280: God's Love and Kindness   282

Prayer 281: God's Strength in My Weakness   283

Prayer 282: God's Goodness in Every Situation   284

Prayer 283: God's Presence in Every Storm   285

Prayer 284: God's Faithfulness in Every Trial   286

Prayer 285: God's Love in My Life   287

Prayer 286: God's Wisdom in My Decisions   288

Prayer 287: God's Assurance of His Presence   289

Prayer 288: God's Peace in My Heart   290

Prayer 289: God's Guidance in My Journey   291

Prayer 290: God's Strength in Adversity   292

Prayer 291: God's Assurance of His Guidance   293

Prayer 292: God's Comfort in Grief   294

Prayer 293: God's Faithfulness in Every Season   295

Prayer 294: God's Joy in My Heart   296

Prayer 295: God's Protection Over My Life   297

Prayer 296: God's Assurance of His Love   298

Prayer 297: God's Goodness in My Life   299

Prayer 298: God's Peace in My Heart   300

Prayer 299: God's Wisdom in My Decisions   301

Prayer 300: God's Faithfulness in Every Season   302

Prayer 301: God's Comfort in Times of Distress   303

Prayer 302: God's Assurance of His Promises   304

Prayer 303: God's Healing in My Life   305

Prayer 304: God's Joy in My Life   306

Prayer 305: God's Faithfulness in My Journey   307

Prayer 306: God's Strength in My Challenges   308

Prayer 307: God's Wisdom in My Decisions   309

Prayer 308: God's Promise of Hope   310

Prayer 309: God's Comfort in My Life   311

Prayer 310: God's Guidance in My Journey   312

Prayer 311: God's Restoration in My Life   313

Prayer 312: God's Faithfulness Through Trials   314

Prayer 313: God's Joy in My Life   315

Prayer 314: God's Peace in My Heart   316

Prayer 315: God's Strength in My Weakness   317

Prayer 316: God's Goodness in My Life   318

Prayer 317: God's Faithfulness in Every Season   319

Prayer 318: God's Hope for the Future   320

Prayer 319: God's Assurance of His Presence   321

Prayer 320: God's Love in My Life   322

Prayer 321: God's Guidance in My Life   323

Prayer 322: God's Peace in Every Situation   324

Prayer 323: God's Strength in Adversity   325

Prayer 324: God's Promise of Restoration 326

Prayer 325: God's Goodness in Every Season 327

Prayer 326: God's Joy in My Heart 328

Prayer 327: God's Assurance in Uncertainty 329

Prayer 328: God's Faithfulness Through Every Trial 330

Prayer 329: God's Love in My Relationships 331

Prayer 330: God's Comfort in Times of Trouble 332

Prayer 331: God's Healing Touch 333

Prayer 332: God's Assurance of His Goodness 334

Prayer 333: God's Strength in Every Challenge 335

Prayer 334: God's Comfort in My Pain 336

Prayer 335: God's Guidance in Every Decision 337

Prayer 336: God's Peace in My Life 338

Prayer 337: God's Love is Unchanging 339

Prayer 338: God's Restoration in My Life 340

Prayer 339: God's Joy in My Heart 341

Prayer 340: God's Assurance in Every Trial 342

Prayer 341: God's Love in Every Situation 343

Prayer 342: God's Peace in Turbulent Times 344

Prayer 343: God's Guidance on My Path 345

Prayer 344: God's Restoration in My Life 346

Prayer 345: God's Strength in Every Trial 347

Prayer 346: God's Joy in My Heart 348

Prayer 347: God's Protection Over My Life 349

Prayer 348: God's Assurance of His Presence 350

Prayer 349: God's Love in My Life 351

Prayer 350: God's Goodness in My Life 352

Prayer 351: God's Strength in My Trials 353

Prayer 352: God's Comfort in Sorrow 354

Prayer 353: God's Wisdom in Every Decision 355

Prayer 354: God's Joy in My Heart   356

Prayer 355: God's Protection Over My Life   357

Prayer 356: God's Assurance of His Love   358

Prayer 357: God's Faithfulness in Every Challenge   359

Prayer 358: God's Restoration in My Life   360

Prayer 359: God's Joy in My Life   361

Prayer 360: God's Assurance in Every Situation   362

Prayer 361: God's Strength in My Weakness   363

Prayer 362: God's Comfort in Times of Distress   364

Prayer 363: God's Assurance of His Guidance   365

Prayer 364: God's Peace in Every Storm   366

Prayer 365: God's Love Endures Forever   367

Reader's Prayer   368

Final Word of Encouragement   369

Introduction:
The Power of Prayer

Prayer is a profound and sacred communication with God, a dialogue that fosters a personal relationship between the believer and the Creator. It is defined as the act of speaking to God, expressing our thoughts, feelings, desires, and needs, while also listening for His guidance and wisdom. Through prayer, we acknowledge our dependence on God and invite His presence into our lives.

Why We Should Pray

Prayer is essential for several reasons. First and foremost, it is a means of deepening our relationship with God. Just as communication is vital in any relationship, prayer allows us to connect with God on a personal level, expressing our gratitude, seeking forgiveness, and laying bare our hearts. Additionally, prayer provides a sense of peace and comfort, reminding us that we are never alone in our struggles. In moments of uncertainty or fear, turning to prayer can bring clarity and reassurance as we place our trust in God's plans.

The Importance of Prayer for a Believer

For believers, prayer is not merely a ritual; it is a lifeline. It serves as a source of strength, guidance, and inspiration. Through prayer, we align our hearts with God's will, seeking His purpose in our lives. It is also a powerful tool for intercession, allowing us to lift up the needs of others and the world around us. In praying for others, we participate in God's work, demonstrating love and compassion.

Moreover, prayer equips us to navigate life's challenges with resilience. It fosters spiritual growth, allowing us to reflect on our relationship with God and encouraging us to cultivate a life of faith. When we pray, we invite God's presence into our circumstances, acknowledging His sovereignty over our lives.

In this "EveryDay is Christmas" prayer book, you will find a collection of prayers designed to inspire, encourage, and strengthen your faith. May these prayers serve as a reminder of the power and importance of prayer in your daily life, drawing you closer to God and filling your heart with His peace, joy, and love.

Prayer 1: God's Unfailing Love

Scripture:

"The Lord has appeared of old to me, saying: 'Yes, I have loved you with an everlasting love; therefore with lovingkindness I have drawn you.'"

(Jeremiah 31:3 NKJV)

Prayer:

Father, I thank You for Your everlasting love. From generation to generation, Your love endures, never failing and never growing weak. I stand in awe of Your lovingkindness that continually draws me closer to You. Help me to live each day in the knowledge of how deeply I am loved by You.

Lord, when I feel distant or unloved, remind me of Your unchanging love. Let Your love be the anchor of my soul, holding me firm through every season of life. I ask that You fill my heart with this love so that I may extend it to others. Thank You, Lord, for loving me with an everlasting love. In the mighty and matchless name of Jesus, I pray, Amen.

Prayer 2: The God Who Sees Me

Scripture:

"Then she called the name of the Lord who spoke to her, You-Are-the-God-Who-Sees; for she said, 'Have I also here seen Him who sees me?'"

(Genesis 16:13 NKJV)

Prayer:

Lord, I thank You for being the God who sees me. In every moment of my life, You are watching over me, knowing my thoughts, my fears, and my struggles. I am never hidden from You, and I find comfort in the knowledge that You are always aware of my situation.

Father, when I feel unseen or overlooked by others, remind me that You see me. Let me find peace and confidence in Your gaze, knowing that I am always in Your care. Help me to live with the awareness that Your eyes are upon me, guiding and protecting me every step of the way.

Thank You, Lord, for being the God who sees me. In the mighty and matchless name of Jesus, I pray, Amen.

Prayer 3: Rest for the Weary

Scripture:

"Come to Me, all you who labor and are heavy laden, and I will give you rest."

(Matthew 11:28 NKJV)

Prayer:

Lord, I thank You for the invitation to find rest in You. When I am burdened and weary from the trials of life, I know that I can come to You and find peace. You alone offer the kind of rest that refreshes my soul and restores my spirit. I come to You today, laying my burdens down at Your feet.

Father, when I am overwhelmed by the pressures of life, help me to remember Your promise of rest. Teach me to rely on You, knowing that You care for me and that You desire to give me peace and renewal.

Thank You, Lord, for the rest You provide. In the mighty and matchless name of Jesus, I pray, Amen.

Prayer 4: Strength in Times of Trouble

Scripture:

"God is our refuge and strength, a very present help in trouble."

(Psalm 46:1 NKJV)

Prayer:

Father, I thank You for being my refuge and strength. In times of trouble, I know that I can run to You and find safety. You are always present, always near, ready to help me when I call on You. Help me to trust in Your strength, knowing that You are my protector and defender.

Lord, when trouble surrounds me, remind me that You are my refuge. Let me find peace in Your presence, confident that You are fighting for me and holding me securely in Your hands.

Thank You, Lord, for being my strength in every trial. In the mighty and matchless name of Jesus, I pray, Amen.

Prayer 5: God's Grace in My Weakness

Scripture:

"And He said to me, 'My grace is sufficient for you, for My strength is made perfect in weakness.' Therefore most gladly I will rather boast in my infirmities, that the power of Christ may rest upon me."

(2 Corinthians 12:9 NKJV)

Prayer:

Lord, I thank You for Your all-sufficient grace. In my moments of weakness, I know that Your strength is made perfect. I ask for Your grace to fill every area of my life where I feel weak or inadequate. Let Your power rest upon me, so that I may walk in victory, even in the midst of challenges.

Father, teach me to rely on Your grace daily, knowing that it is more than enough for every situation. Help me to embrace my weakness, trusting that Your strength will shine through and accomplish what I cannot.

Thank You, Lord, for Your grace that never fails. In the mighty and matchless name of Jesus, I pray, Amen.

Prayer 6: The Light of the World

Scripture:

"Then Jesus spoke to them again, saying, 'I am the light of the world. He who follows Me shall not walk in darkness, but have the light of life.'"

(John 8:12 NKJV)

Prayer:

Father, I thank You for sending Jesus, the light of the world. In Him, I have found the light of life, and I no longer have to walk in darkness. Help me to follow closely after Jesus, allowing His light to guide my steps and illuminate my path.

Lord, when darkness surrounds me or when I feel lost, remind me that I have the light of life within me. Let Your light shine through me, bringing hope and clarity to every area of my life. May I also be a light to others, reflecting Your love and truth.

Thank You, Lord, for being the light that leads me out of darkness. In the mighty and matchless name of Jesus, I pray, Amen.

Prayer 7: God's Faithfulness to Keep His Promises

Scripture:

"For He who promised is faithful."

(Hebrews 10:23 NKJV)

Prayer:

Lord, I thank You for Your faithfulness to keep every promise. You are not a man that You should lie, and I trust that every word You have spoken will come to pass. Help me to hold fast to the hope I have in You, without wavering, for I know that You are faithful.

Father, when I am tempted to doubt or grow impatient, remind me of Your track record of faithfulness. Let me rest in the assurance that You are always true to Your Word, and that what You have promised, You will fulfill.

Thank You, Lord, for being faithful in every situation. In the mighty and matchless name of Jesus, I pray, Amen.

Prayer 8: Trusting God's Timing

Scripture:

"He has made everything beautiful in its time. Also, He has put eternity in their hearts, except that no one can find out the work that God does from beginning to end."
(Ecclesiastes 3:11 NKJV)

Prayer:

Father, I thank You for Your perfect timing. Even when I cannot see the full picture, I trust that You are working all things for good. Help me to be patient in the waiting, knowing that You make everything beautiful in its time.

Lord, when I am anxious about the future or frustrated by delays, remind me that Your timing is always best. Teach me to trust in Your wisdom and to rest in the assurance that You are working behind the scenes for my benefit.

Thank You, Lord, for Your divine timing. In the mighty and matchless name of Jesus, I pray, Amen.

Prayer 9: Peace in the Storm

Scripture:

"Then He arose and rebuked the wind, and said to the sea, 'Peace, be still!' And the wind ceased and there was a great calm."

(Mark 4:39 NKJV)

Prayer:

Lord, I thank You for the peace that only You can give. Just as You calmed the storm on the sea, I ask that You bring peace to any storms in my life today. Speak to the wind and the waves, and let Your peace bring a great calm to my heart.

Father, when I feel overwhelmed or afraid, remind me that You are with me in the midst of the storm. Let me find rest in Your presence, knowing that You are greater than any challenge or trial I may face.

Thank You, Lord, for the peace that stills every storm. In the mighty and matchless name of Jesus, I pray, Amen.

Prayer 10: God's Guidance in Every Decision

Scripture:

"Trust in the Lord with all your heart, and lean not on your own understanding; in all your ways acknowledge Him, and He shall direct your paths."

(Proverbs 3:5-6 NKJV)

Prayer:

Lord, I thank You for Your guidance and direction in my life. When I trust in You and acknowledge You in all my ways, You promise to direct my steps. Help me to lean on Your wisdom and not on my own understanding, knowing that Your ways are higher than mine.

Father, when I face difficult decisions, remind me to seek You first. Let Your Word be my guide, and help me to follow the path You have set before me with confidence and faith. Thank You, Lord, for leading me in the right direction. In the mighty and matchless name of Jesus, I pray, Amen.

Prayer 11: God, My Ever-Present Help

Scripture:

"The Lord is near to all who call upon Him, to all who call upon Him in truth."

(Psalm 145:18 NKJV)

Prayer:

Father, I thank You for always being near to me. Whenever I call on You, You hear me, and You are ready to respond with love and care. Today, I come before You with a heart that seeks Your presence. I need You, Lord, and I am grateful that I can reach out to You in my time of need.

Lord, sometimes I feel distant, overwhelmed by life's pressures, but I know that You are never far. Help me to remember that You are always close, waiting for me to call upon You with a sincere heart. Let me trust in Your nearness and rest in Your peace.

Thank You, Lord, for being my ever-present help. In the mighty and matchless name of Jesus, I pray, Amen.

Prayer 12: Trusting in God's Faithfulness

Scripture:

"Let us hold fast the confession of our hope without wavering, for He who promised is faithful."

(Hebrews 10:23 NKJV)

Prayer:

Lord, I thank You for Your faithfulness. In moments when doubt tries to creep in, I remind myself that You are always true to Your word. You have promised to never leave me nor forsake me, and I hold tightly to that truth today. Help me, Lord, not to waver in my faith, but to stand firm in the hope that You have given me.

Father, when I face situations that test my faith, remind me of Your past faithfulness. Let me see how You have worked in my life before, and help me to trust that You will do it again. I know that every promise You have made, You will keep.

Thank You, Lord, for being so faithful to me. In the mighty and matchless name of Jesus, I pray, Amen.

Prayer 13: Peace Beyond Understanding

Scripture:

"And the peace of God, which surpasses all understanding, will guard your hearts and minds through Christ Jesus."
(Philippians 4:7 NKJV)

Prayer:

Father, I thank You for the peace that goes beyond what I can comprehend. There are times when the world around me feels chaotic, but You offer me a peace that stands firm no matter what. Today, I ask for that peace to fill my heart and mind. Guard me, Lord, from the worries that try to steal my joy and rest.

Lord, when I'm overwhelmed by circumstances, remind me to look to You. Help me to surrender my anxieties and fears to You, knowing that Your peace is stronger than any storm I face. Let my heart be still, trusting in Your protection.

Thank You, Lord, for Your peace that surpasses all understanding. In the mighty and matchless name of Jesus, I pray, Amen.

Prayer 14: Renew My Strength, Lord

Scripture:

"But those who wait on the Lord shall renew their strength; they shall mount up with wings like eagles, they shall run and not be weary, they shall walk and not faint."
(Isaiah 40:31 NKJV)

Prayer:

Father, I come to You weary, but I trust in Your promise to renew my strength. I know that as I wait on You, You will lift me up and give me the energy I need to continue. Help me to be patient in the waiting, knowing that You are working even when I can't see it.

Let my heart be renewed as I place my trust in You. Lord, when I feel like giving up, remind me that You are my strength. Let me soar like an eagle, running this race with endurance, not growing weary or fainting. I believe that You are more than able to sustain me through every challenge. Thank You, Lord, for renewing my strength. In the mighty and matchless name of Jesus, I pray, Amen.

Prayer 15: God's Plans Are Perfect

Scripture:

"For I know the thoughts that I think toward you, says the Lord, thoughts of peace and not of evil, to give you a future and a hope."

(Jeremiah 29:11 NKJV)

Prayer:

Lord, I thank You that Your plans for me are good. Sometimes, I worry about the future, but I am comforted knowing that You have a plan for my life—a plan full of hope and peace. Help me to trust in Your perfect will, even when I don't understand what's ahead. I know that You have my best interests at heart.

Father, when I am anxious about tomorrow, remind me that You are already there, preparing the way for me. Help me to rest in the assurance that Your plans are better than anything I could imagine. Let me walk confidently into the future, knowing that You are with me.

Thank You, Lord, for the hope and future You have promised me. In the mighty and matchless name of Jesus, I pray, Amen.

Prayer 16: God, My Shield and Defender

Scripture:

"But You, O Lord, are a shield for me, my glory and the One who lifts up my head."

(Psalm 3:3 NKJV)

Prayer:

Father, I thank You for being my shield and my defender. In times of trouble, You are the One who lifts my head and gives me hope. When the enemy comes against me, I trust that You are protecting me and fighting on my behalf. I don't have to fear, because You are my refuge.

Lord, when I feel attacked or surrounded by difficulties, help me to remember that You are my shield. Lift my head when I am downcast, and remind me that I am never alone. I am safe in Your care, and nothing can harm me outside of Your will.

Thank You, Lord, for being my defender. In the mighty and matchless name of Jesus, I pray, Amen.

Prayer 17: Confidence in God's Timing

Scripture:

"He has made everything beautiful in its time."
(Ecclesiastes 3:11 NKJV)

Prayer:

Father, I thank You for the beauty of Your perfect timing. Sometimes, I want things to happen on my schedule, but I know that Your timing is always better. Help me to trust in the process, knowing that You are making everything beautiful in Your time. Let my heart be patient and confident in Your timing.

Lord, when I am tempted to rush ahead or become frustrated by delays, remind me that You are in control. Teach me to rest in the assurance that You are working all things together for good, even when I can't see it yet.

Thank You, Lord, for making everything beautiful in Your time. In the mighty and matchless name of Jesus, I pray, Amen.

Prayer 18: Walking by Faith

Scripture:

"For we walk by faith, not by sight."

(2 Corinthians 5:7 NKJV)

Prayer:

Lord, I thank You for teaching me to walk by faith and not by sight. Even when I don't see the full picture or understand the journey ahead, I trust that You are leading me. Help me to take steps of faith, knowing that You are guiding me every step of the way.

Father, when I am afraid to move forward, remind me that faith is believing in what I cannot see. Strengthen my trust in You, and let my walk be a testimony of Your faithfulness. I choose to walk by faith today, trusting in Your promises.

Thank You, Lord, for giving me the courage to walk by faith. In the mighty and matchless name of Jesus, I pray, Amen.

Prayer 19: God's Unshakable Word

Scripture:

"Heaven and earth will pass away, but My words will by no means pass away."
(Matthew 24:35 NKJV)

Prayer:

Lord, I thank You for the power and permanence of Your Word. In a world that is constantly changing, Your Word remains the same. Help me to build my life on the firm foundation of Your promises, knowing that they will never fail or fade. Let Your truth be the guide that leads me in every season.

Father, when I am faced with uncertainty or doubt, remind me that Your Word is unshakable. Let me cling to Your promises, trusting that they are true and eternal. No matter what happens around me, Your Word remains.

Thank You, Lord, for Your unchanging Word. In the mighty and matchless name of Jesus, I pray, Amen.

Prayer 20: God's Light in My Darkness

Scripture:

"Your word is a lamp to my feet and a light to my path."
(Psalm 119:105 NKJV)

Prayer:

Father, I thank You for the light of Your Word that guides my steps. When I don't know which way to go, Your Word illuminates the path ahead of me. Help me to rely on Your Word for direction, trusting that it will always lead me in the right way.

Lord, when I feel lost or unsure of the next step, remind me to turn to Your Word. Let it be the light that shows me the way forward. Help me to walk in obedience to Your truth, knowing that it will lead me safely to where You want me to be.

Thank You, Lord, for the light of Your Word in my life. In the mighty and matchless name of Jesus, I pray, Amen.

Prayer 21: Strength in My Weakness

Scripture:

"The Lord is my strength and my shield; my heart trusted in Him, and I am helped; therefore my heart greatly rejoices, and with my song I will praise Him."

(Psalm 28:7 NKJV)

Prayer:

Lord, I thank You for being my strength when I am weak. You are my shield, and because of You, I am helped. I place my trust in You today, knowing that You are more than able to sustain me. When I feel overwhelmed, remind me to lean on Your strength and not my own.

Father, fill my heart with joy, even in the midst of difficulty, because I know that You are with me. Let my heart sing praises to You as I reflect on Your faithfulness. You have never failed me, and I know You never will.

Thank You, Lord, for being my strength and my shield. In the mighty and matchless name of Jesus, I pray, Amen.

Prayer 22: Living in God's Freedom

Scripture:

"Stand fast therefore in the liberty by which Christ has made us free, and do not be entangled again with a yoke of bondage."

(*Galatians 5:1 NKJV*)

Prayer:

Father, I thank You for the freedom I have in Christ. Because of Him, I no longer have to live in the bondage of sin or fear. Help me to stand firm in the liberty You have given me and to reject anything that tries to pull me back into captivity.

Lord, when I feel tempted to fall into old patterns, remind me that I am free in You. Let me walk in the confidence of that freedom, trusting that You have broken every chain and set me free for a purpose.

Thank You, Lord, for the freedom I have through Jesus. In the mighty and matchless name of Jesus, I pray, Amen.

Prayer 23: God, My Refuge and Strength

Scripture:

"The name of the Lord is a strong tower; the righteous run to it and are safe."

(Proverbs 18:10 NKJV)

Prayer:

Father, I thank You for being my refuge, my strong tower. In times of trouble, I can run to You and find safety. Your name alone is a shield that protects me from harm. Today, I choose to rest in the security of Your name, knowing that I am safe in Your care.

Lord, when fear or uncertainty tries to creep in, remind me that I can always call on You. Let my heart be anchored in Your protection, and let me run to You in every situation. You are my safe place, and I trust You completely.

Thank You, Lord, for being my refuge and my strength. In the mighty and matchless name of Jesus, I pray, Amen.

Prayer 24: God's Grace to Forgive

Scripture:

"And be kind to one another, tenderhearted, forgiving one another, even as God in Christ forgave you."
(Ephesians 4:32 NKJV)

Prayer:

Lord, I thank You for the forgiveness I have received through Christ. Help me to extend that same forgiveness to others, even when it's hard. Soften my heart, and let me be kind and tenderhearted, just as You have been with me.

Father, when I struggle to forgive, remind me of the mercy You've shown me. Let me not hold onto bitterness, but release it in favor of love and grace. Help me to reflect Your love in my relationships, choosing forgiveness over resentment.

Thank You, Lord, for teaching me to forgive as You have forgiven me. In the mighty and matchless name of Jesus, I pray, Amen.

Prayer 25: Trusting in God's Faithfulness

Scripture:

"Know therefore that the Lord your God, He is God, the faithful God who keeps covenant and mercy for a thousand generations with those who love Him and keep His commandments."

(Deuteronomy 7:9 NKJV)

Prayer:

Father, I thank You for being the faithful God who keeps Your promises. You are unchanging, and I can trust You completely. Help me to remember Your faithfulness, especially when I face uncertain times. Let me rest in the assurance that You are always true to Your word.

Lord, when doubt tries to take root in my heart, remind me of Your covenant. Help me to walk in obedience to You, trusting that You will always be faithful to keep Your promises.

Thank You, Lord, for Your everlasting faithfulness. In the mighty and matchless name of Jesus, I pray, Amen.

Prayer 26: God's Healing Touch

Scripture:

"But He was wounded for our transgressions, He was bruised for our iniquities; the chastisement for our peace was upon Him, and by His stripes we are healed."
(Isaiah 53:5 NKJV)

Prayer:

Lord, I thank You for the healing that comes through Jesus. Because of His sacrifice, I can experience healing—physically, emotionally, and spiritually. Today, I ask for Your healing touch in my life. Where there is pain or brokenness, I trust in Your power to restore and make whole.

Father, when I feel weak or discouraged, remind me of the price that was paid for my healing. Let me walk in the confidence that by His stripes, I am healed. I trust You to heal every area of my life that needs Your touch.

Thank You, Lord, for being my healer. In the mighty and matchless name of Jesus, I pray, Amen.

Prayer 27: Walking in God's Wisdom

Scripture:

"If any of you lacks wisdom, let him ask of God, who gives to all liberally and without reproach, and it will be given to him."

(James 1:5 NKJV)

Prayer:

Father, I thank You for the promise of wisdom. Whenever I am unsure or lacking understanding, I can come to You, and You will generously provide the wisdom I need. Today, I ask for Your wisdom to guide my decisions, thoughts, and actions.

Lord, when I am faced with difficult choices, remind me to seek Your wisdom above my own. Let Your Spirit guide me in truth, so that I may walk in a way that honors You. Help me to trust in Your perfect wisdom, knowing that You see the bigger picture.

Thank You, Lord, for giving me the wisdom I need each day. In the mighty and matchless name of Jesus, I pray, Amen.

Prayer 28: God's Promise of Peace

Scripture:

"You will keep him in perfect peace, whose mind is stayed on You, because he trusts in You."

(Isaiah 26:3 NKJV)

Prayer:

Lord, I thank You for the perfect peace that comes from trusting in You. Today, I fix my mind on You, knowing that in Your presence, there is peace that surpasses all understanding. Let my heart rest in Your peace, no matter what circumstances I face.

Father, when worry or fear tries to take hold of me, remind me to focus on You. Let Your peace guard my heart and mind, bringing calm in the midst of chaos. Help me to trust in Your faithfulness, knowing that You are in control.

Thank You, Lord, for Your perfect peace. In the mighty and matchless name of Jesus, I pray, Amen.

Prayer 29: God's Mercy Endures Forever

Scripture:

"Oh, give thanks to the Lord, for He is good! For His mercy endures forever."

(Psalm 136:1 NKJV)

Prayer:

Father, I thank You for Your goodness and mercy that never end. Your love is unchanging, and Your mercy is fresh every morning. Today, I give You thanks for the many ways You have shown me mercy, even when I didn't deserve it.

Lord, help me to live in gratitude for the mercy You extend to me each day. Let me never take it for granted but always be aware of Your kindness and grace. Fill my heart with thanksgiving, knowing that Your mercy endures forever.

Thank You, Lord, for Your everlasting mercy. In the mighty and matchless name of Jesus, I pray, Amen.

Prayer 30: God's Power at Work in Me

Scripture:

"Now to Him who is able to do exceedingly abundantly above all that we ask or think, according to the power that works in us."

(Ephesians 3:20 NKJV)

Prayer:

Lord, I thank You for the power at work within me. You are able to do far more than I can ask, think, or imagine, and I trust in Your power to work in my life. Help me to believe for the impossible, knowing that with You, all things are possible.

Father, when I face challenges or obstacles, remind me that Your power is at work in me. Let me trust in Your ability to accomplish more than I can even dream of. Increase my faith, and let me see Your hand moving in miraculous ways.

Thank You, Lord, for the power You have placed within me. In the mighty and matchless name of Jesus, I pray, Amen.

Prayer 31: The Lord Is My Shepherd

Scripture:

"The Lord is my shepherd; I shall not want."
(Psalm 23:1 NKJV)

Prayer:

Father, I thank You for being my Shepherd, always caring for my needs. In You, I lack nothing. You provide for me, lead me, and guide me into the paths of righteousness. Help me to trust Your leadership, knowing that You are always looking out for me.

Lord, when I am unsure of what lies ahead, remind me that You are guiding me every step of the way. I find peace and rest in Your care, knowing that I am never without what I need because You are with me.

Thank You, Lord, for being my faithful Shepherd. In the mighty and matchless name of Jesus, I pray, Amen.

Prayer 32: Walking in Love

Scripture:

"And walk in love, as Christ also has loved us and given Himself for us, an offering and a sacrifice to God for a sweet-smelling aroma."

(Ephesians 5:2 NKJV)

Prayer:

Father, I thank You for the love You have shown me through Jesus Christ. Help me to walk in that same love each day, offering kindness, forgiveness, and compassion to those around me. Let my actions be a reflection of the love Christ demonstrated on the cross.

Lord, when it's difficult to love, give me the grace to do so anyway. Teach me to love as You love, even those who may not be easy to love. Let my life be a sweet-smelling aroma to You, an offering of love that brings You glory.

Thank You, Lord, for empowering me to walk in love. In the mighty and matchless name of Jesus, I pray, Amen.

Prayer 33: God's Strength in the Battle

Scripture:

"The Lord is a man of war; the Lord is His name."
(Exodus 15:3 NKJV)

Prayer:

Father, I thank You that You fight my battles for me. You are the Lord of hosts, mighty in battle, and I place my trust in You when the enemy comes against me. Teach me to stand firm in faith, knowing that You are fighting on my behalf.

Lord, when I feel weak or afraid, remind me that You are my strength. I don't have to fight alone because You are always with me, leading me to victory. Help me to stand in Your power and not my own.

Thank You, Lord, for being my warrior and my defender. In the mighty and matchless name of Jesus, I pray, Amen.

Prayer 34: God's Peace in the Waiting

Scripture:

"Wait on the Lord; be of good courage, and He shall strengthen your heart; wait, I say, on the Lord!"
(Psalm 27:14 NKJV)

Prayer:

Lord, I thank You for the strength that comes from waiting on You. Sometimes, the waiting is hard, but I trust that You are working in the unseen. Teach me to be patient and courageous as I wait for Your promises to unfold in my life.

Father, when I grow weary or anxious, remind me that waiting on You is never wasted time. Strengthen my heart and fill me with peace as I place my trust in Your perfect timing.

Thank You, Lord, for the peace You give in the waiting. In the mighty and matchless name of Jesus, I pray, Amen.

Prayer 35: Guarding My Heart

Scripture:

"Keep your heart with all diligence, for out of it spring the issues of life."

(Proverbs 4:23 NKJV)

Prayer:

Father, I thank You for reminding me to guard my heart, for it is the wellspring of life. Help me to be mindful of what I allow into my heart—whether through thoughts, words, or actions. I ask for Your protection over my heart so that I may live according to Your will.

Lord, when negativity, doubt, or temptation try to take root in my heart, give me the wisdom and strength to reject them. Let me fill my heart with Your Word and Your truth, so that what flows from me is pleasing to You.

Thank You, Lord, for helping me guard my heart. In the mighty and matchless name of Jesus, I pray, Amen.

Prayer 36: God's Compassion for the Weary

Scripture:

"He gives power to the weak, and to those who have no might He increases strength."

(Isaiah 40:29 NKJV)

Prayer:

Lord, I thank You for Your compassion toward those who are weak and weary. When I feel like I have nothing left to give, I know that You are the One who strengthens me. I come to You today, asking for a fresh outpouring of Your strength and grace.

Father, when my heart is heavy or my body is tired, remind me that You are my source of power. You never grow weary, and You are always ready to lift me up. I rely on Your strength today, knowing that You will carry me through.

Thank You, Lord, for increasing my strength when I am weak. In the mighty and matchless name of Jesus, I pray, Amen.

Prayer 37: Embracing God's Grace

Scripture:

"And of His fullness we have all received, and grace for grace."

(John 1:16 NKJV)

Prayer:

Father, I thank You for the grace You have given me, grace upon grace. Your love for me is so abundant, and Your grace never runs out. Help me to embrace that grace each day, knowing that I am forgiven, redeemed, and loved by You.

Lord, when I feel unworthy or overwhelmed by my failures, remind me of the fullness of Your grace. Let me walk in the freedom that Your grace provides, and let that grace flow through me to others.

Thank You, Lord, for Your endless grace. In the mighty and matchless name of Jesus, I pray, Amen.

Prayer 38: Walking in Righteousness

Scripture:

"Blessed are those who hunger and thirst for righteousness, for they shall be filled."

(Matthew 5:6 NKJV)

Prayer:

Lord, I thank You for giving me a heart that longs for righteousness. I want to live a life that pleases You, and I ask that You fill me with a deep hunger for Your truth and Your ways. Let my desire for righteousness grow stronger every day.

Father, when the world tempts me with distractions or sin, remind me of the joy that comes from walking in righteousness. Fill me with Your Spirit and empower me to live a life that honors You.

Thank You, Lord, for filling me as I seek after righteousness. In the mighty and matchless name of Jesus, I pray, Amen.

Prayer 39: Trusting God in the Unknown

Scripture:

"I will go before you and make the crooked places straight; I will break in pieces the gates of bronze and cut the bars of iron."

(Isaiah 45:2 NKJV)

Prayer:

Father, I thank You for going before me and making the way clear. Even when I can't see the full path ahead, I trust that You are already there, straightening the crooked places and breaking down barriers. Help me to walk in faith, knowing that You are guiding me through the unknown.

Lord, when fear of the future tries to creep in, remind me that You are my guide and my protector. I don't have to know everything because You do, and I trust that You are leading me to where I need to be.

Thank You, Lord, for making a way for me. In the mighty and matchless name of Jesus, I pray, Amen.

Prayer 40: God's Everlasting Covenant

Scripture:

"I will make an everlasting covenant with them, that I will not turn away from doing them good; but I will put My fear in their hearts so that they will not depart from Me."
(Jeremiah 32:40 NKJV)

Prayer:

Lord, I thank You for the everlasting covenant You have made with me. Your promises are eternal, and You have committed to doing good for me all the days of my life. Help me to hold fast to this covenant, trusting in Your goodness and faithfulness.

Father, put a holy reverence for You in my heart so that I will never depart from Your ways. Let me walk in the fullness of Your promises, knowing that You are always working for my good.

Thank You, Lord, for Your everlasting covenant of love and grace. In the mighty and matchless name of Jesus, I pray, Amen.

Prayer 41: God's Light That Shines in the Darkness

Scripture:

"The light shines in the darkness, and the darkness has not overcome it."

(John 1:5 NKJV)

Prayer:

Father, I thank You for the light of Christ that shines in the darkest places. No matter how deep the darkness, it can never overcome Your light. Today, I ask that You fill me with Your light, so that I may reflect it to those around me.

Lord, when I feel surrounded by darkness or fear, remind me that Your light is always with me. Let Your presence drive away every shadow, and let me walk confidently in the truth that Your light cannot be extinguished.

Thank You, Lord, for being the light in my life. In the mighty and matchless name of Jesus, I pray, Amen.

Prayer 42: God's Wisdom in Every Decision

Scripture:

"Trust in the Lord with all your heart, and lean not on your own understanding; in all your ways acknowledge Him, and He shall direct your paths."

(Proverbs 3:5-6 NKJV)

Prayer:

Father, I thank You for the wisdom You provide when I trust in You. So often I try to figure things out on my own, but today I choose to lean on You completely. I surrender my plans, my thoughts, and my decisions to You, trusting that You will direct my paths.

Lord, when I am faced with uncertainty or confusion, remind me to turn to You first. Help me not to rely on my own understanding but to acknowledge You in every area of my life. I know that as I trust You, You will lead me in the way I should go.

Thank You, Lord, for Your wisdom and guidance. In the mighty and matchless name of Jesus, I pray, Amen.

Prayer 43: Trusting in God's Protection

Scripture:

"The Lord is my rock and my fortress and my deliverer; My God, my strength, in whom I will trust; my shield and the horn of my salvation, my stronghold."

(Psalm 18:2 NKJV)

Prayer:

Lord, I thank You for being my rock and fortress. In You, I am safe from all harm, and I trust in Your protection over my life. You are my strength and my deliverer, and I have no reason to fear because I am under Your care.

Father, when I feel vulnerable or afraid, remind me that You are my shield and stronghold. Let me find comfort in Your presence, knowing that You surround me with Your mighty power. Help me to stand firm in faith, trusting that nothing can touch me outside of Your will.

Thank You, Lord, for being my refuge and protection. In the mighty and matchless name of Jesus, I pray, Amen.

Prayer 44: God's Joy is My Strength

Scripture:

"The joy of the Lord is your strength."
                                    (Nehemiah 8:10 NKJV)

Prayer:

Father, I thank You for the joy that comes from knowing You. In times of difficulty, it is Your joy that strengthens me and carries me through. Help me to hold onto that joy, no matter what circumstances I face, knowing that it is not dependent on my situation but on my relationship with You.

Lord, when I feel weak or overwhelmed, remind me that Your joy is my strength. Let me draw from the well of joy You have placed in my heart, and let it be a source of peace, comfort, and power in every season of life.

Thank You, Lord, for the strength that comes from Your joy. In the mighty and matchless name of Jesus, I pray, Amen.

Prayer 45: Trusting God to Provide

Scripture:

"And my God shall supply all your need according to His riches in glory by Christ Jesus."

(Philippians 4:19 NKJV)

Prayer:

Father, I thank You for being my provider. In every season of life, You have supplied all of my needs, and I trust You to continue to do so. I come to You today, laying my concerns at Your feet, knowing that You will provide according to Your glorious riches in Christ Jesus.

Lord, when I am tempted to worry or fear about lack, remind me of Your faithfulness. Help me to trust that You are more than able to meet my every need, and teach me to live with a heart full of gratitude, knowing that You are always taking care of me.

Thank You, Lord, for Your faithful provision. In the mighty and matchless name of Jesus, I pray, Amen.

Prayer 46: God's Grace is Sufficient

Scripture:

"And He said to me, 'My grace is sufficient for you, for My strength is made perfect in weakness.' Therefore most gladly I will rather boast in my infirmities, that the power of Christ may rest upon me."

(2 Corinthians 12:9 NKJV)

Prayer:

Lord, I thank You for Your grace that is always enough. In moments when I feel weak or inadequate, I know that Your strength is made perfect in me. Help me to embrace my weaknesses, knowing that they allow Your power to shine through me.

Father, when I feel like I can't go on, remind me that Your grace will carry me through. Let me rely on You, not on my own strength, trusting that Your power rests upon me in every circumstance.

Thank You, Lord, for Your all-sufficient grace. In the mighty and matchless name of Jesus, I pray, Amen.

Prayer 47: God's Word Brings Life

Scripture:

"Man shall not live by bread alone, but by every word that proceeds from the mouth of God."

(Matthew 4:4 NKJV)

Prayer:

Father, I thank You for the power of Your Word, which sustains me more than any physical food. Your Word brings life to my spirit and nourishment to my soul. Help me to seek Your Word daily, knowing that it is my source of strength and direction.

Lord, when I feel spiritually empty, remind me to turn to Your Word. Let it fill me with life and truth, guiding my thoughts and actions. Teach me to rely on Your Word above all else, trusting that it will lead me in the way I should go.

Thank You, Lord, for the life-giving power of Your Word. In the mighty and matchless name of Jesus, I pray, Amen.

Prayer 48: Peace in the Midst of the Storm

Scripture:

"And He said to them, 'Why are you so fearful? How is it that you have no faith?' And they feared exceedingly, and said to one another, 'Who can this be, that even the wind and the sea obey Him!'"

(Mark 4:40-41 NKJV)

Prayer:

Father, I thank You for the peace that only You can bring, even in the middle of life's storms. When the wind and waves of life try to overwhelm me, I look to You, the One who commands the storm to be still. Help me to have faith and not fear, knowing that You are in control.

Lord, when I am afraid, remind me of Your power. You are greater than any storm I face, and I trust in Your ability to bring calm to my heart and mind. Let Your peace fill me today, as I rest in Your presence.

Thank You, Lord, for Your peace that surpasses all understanding. In the mighty and matchless name of Jesus, I pray, Amen.

Prayer 49: God's Strength to Overcome Temptation

Scripture:

"No temptation has overtaken you except such as is common to man; but God is faithful, who will not allow you to be tempted beyond what you are able, but with the temptation will also make the way of escape, that you may be able to bear it."

(1 Corinthians 10:13 NKJV)

Prayer:

Lord, I thank You for the strength You provide in times of temptation. I know that I am not alone in my struggles, and that You are faithful to provide a way of escape. Help me to recognize that escape and to walk in victory over the things that try to lead me away from You.

Father, when temptation feels too strong, remind me that You are stronger. Fill me with Your Spirit and empower me to resist the enemy, knowing that You have already made a way for me to overcome.

Thank You, Lord, for Your faithfulness to help me overcome every temptation. In the mighty and matchless name of Jesus, I pray, Amen.

Prayer 50: Restoring My Soul

Scripture:

"He restores my soul; He leads me in the paths of righteousness for His name's sake."

(Psalm 23:3 NKJV)

Prayer:

Father, I thank You for being the One who restores my soul. When I am weary or burdened, You refresh my spirit and lead me in the paths of righteousness. I ask for Your restoration today—renew my heart, mind, and soul so that I may walk in the fullness of Your peace and joy.

Lord, when I feel like I've lost my way, guide me back to the paths You have set before me. Restore what has been broken, and lead me forward with confidence in Your love.

Thank You, Lord, for restoring my soul. In the mighty and matchless name of Jesus, I pray, Amen.

Prayer 51: God's Light in My Darkness

Scripture:

"For You will light my lamp; the Lord my God will enlighten my darkness."

(Psalm 18:28 NKJV)

Prayer:

Father, I thank You for being the light that shines in my darkness. When things seem unclear or overwhelming, You bring clarity and hope. I ask for Your light to guide me today, leading me out of any confusion or fear.

Lord, when I am surrounded by uncertainty, let Your light break through and show me the way forward. Teach me to trust in You, knowing that Your light is stronger than any darkness.

Thank You, Lord, for being the light in my life. In the mighty and matchless name of Jesus, I pray, Amen.

Prayer 52: The Lord Is My Salvation

Scripture:

"The Lord is my light and my salvation; whom shall I fear? The Lord is the strength of my life; of whom shall I be afraid?"

(Psalm 27:1 NKJV)

Prayer:

Lord, I thank You for being my light and my salvation. In You, I find the strength to face anything that comes my way. You have already delivered me from so much, and I trust that You will continue to be my strong tower. Help me to live without fear, knowing that You are with me and for me.

Father, when fear tries to grip my heart, remind me of Your great power and protection. You are the strength of my life, and with You on my side, I have nothing to fear.

Thank You, Lord, for being my salvation and my strength. In the mighty and matchless name of Jesus, I pray, Amen.

Prayer 53: God's Peace to Guard My Heart

Scripture:

"And the peace of God, which surpasses all understanding, will guard your hearts and minds through Christ Jesus."
(Philippians 4:7 NKJV)

Prayer:

Father, I thank You for the peace that only You can provide. Your peace goes beyond anything I can understand, and it protects my heart and mind. Today, I ask for that peace to fill me and guard me against the anxieties and worries that try to overwhelm me.

Lord, when I feel troubled or stressed, remind me to turn to You. Let Your peace be a shield around my heart, calming my fears and bringing rest to my soul. I trust You to keep me in perfect peace as I keep my mind on You.

Thank You, Lord, for Your peace that guards me. In the mighty and matchless name of Jesus, I pray, Amen.

Prayer 54: God's Help in My Time of Need

Scripture:

"Let us therefore come boldly to the throne of grace, that we may obtain mercy and find grace to help in time of need."
(Hebrews 4:16 NKJV)

Prayer:

Lord, I thank You for the privilege of coming boldly before Your throne of grace. I know that I can approach You without fear, knowing that You will meet me with mercy and grace. Today, I come to You in my time of need, asking for Your help, Your guidance, and Your strength.

Father, when I feel unworthy or hesitant to ask for help, remind me that You are my loving Father who is always ready to extend grace. Let me come to You with confidence, trusting that You will provide everything I need.

Thank You, Lord, for Your mercy and grace in every situation. In the mighty and matchless name of Jesus, I pray, Amen.

Prayer 55: New Heart and Spirit

Scripture:

"I will give you a new heart and put a new spirit within you; I will take the heart of stone out of your flesh and give you a heart of flesh."

(Ezekiel 36:26 NKJV)

Prayer:

Father, I thank You for Your transforming power. You have given me a new heart and placed a new spirit within me, changing me from the inside out. Where my heart was once hardened, You have softened it and filled it with Your love. Help me to live with this renewed heart, seeking You in everything I do.

Lord, when I feel distant or disconnected, remind me that You have done a deep work in me. Let my heart remain tender before You, always open to Your leading and filled with Your Spirit.

Thank You, Lord, for giving me a new heart and spirit. In the mighty and matchless name of Jesus, I pray, Amen.

Prayer 56: God's Strength in My Weakness

Scripture:

"He gives power to the weak, and to those who have no might He increases strength."

(Isaiah 40:29 NKJV)

Prayer:

Father, I thank You for being my source of strength when I feel weak. You never leave me in my moments of exhaustion but instead offer me Your power to keep going. Today, I come to You with my weariness, trusting that You will renew my strength.

Lord, when I have no more might of my own, remind me that I don't have to rely on my own power. Let me lean into You, knowing that Your strength is always enough. Fill me with Your strength, so that I can continue to move forward.

Thank You, Lord, for increasing my strength when I need it most. In the mighty and matchless name of Jesus, I pray, Amen.

Prayer 57: God's Faithfulness Through Every Season

Scripture:

"To everything there is a season, a time for every purpose under heaven."

(Ecclesiastes 3:1 NKJV)

Prayer:

Lord, I thank You for Your faithfulness through every season of life. No matter what season I am in—whether joy or sorrow, peace or struggle—I trust that You have a purpose for it. Help me to see Your hand in every season and to rest in the knowledge that You are working all things for good.

Father, when I don't understand why I am going through certain things, remind me that You are in control of the times and seasons. Teach me to trust Your timing and Your plan, knowing that everything has its place in Your greater purpose.

Thank You, Lord, for Your faithfulness in every season. In the mighty and matchless name of Jesus, I pray, Amen.

Prayer 58: God's Healing Power

Scripture:

"Heal me, O Lord, and I shall be healed; save me, and I shall be saved, for You are my praise."

(Jeremiah 17:14 NKJV)

Prayer:

Lord, I thank You for being my healer. You are the One who heals not only my body but also my heart and soul. Today, I bring every area of my life that needs healing before You, trusting that Your power is more than enough to restore me.

Father, when I feel broken or in pain, remind me that You are my great physician. I place my faith in Your ability to heal and make me whole. Let Your healing touch be upon me today, bringing restoration to every area of my life.

Thank You, Lord, for Your healing power. In the mighty and matchless name of Jesus, I pray, Amen.

Prayer 59: Renewing My Mind in Christ

Scripture:

"And do not be conformed to this world, but be transformed by the renewing of your mind, that you may prove what is that good and acceptable and perfect will of God."
(Romans 12:2 NKJV)

Prayer:

Father, I thank You for the renewing of my mind. In a world full of distractions and influences, I choose to fix my thoughts on You. Help me not to conform to the patterns of this world but to be transformed by the renewing of my mind in Christ.

Lord, when my thoughts become clouded with worry, doubt, or fear, remind me to turn to Your Word. Let Your truth fill my mind and shape my decisions so that I may live according to Your perfect will.

Thank You, Lord, for the renewal of my mind. In the mighty and matchless name of Jesus, I pray, Amen.

Prayer 60: God's Strength in Spiritual Battles

Scripture:

"Finally, my brethren, be strong in the Lord and in the power of His might. Put on the whole armor of God, that you may be able to stand against the wiles of the devil."

(Ephesians 6:10-11 NKJV)

Prayer:

Lord, I thank You for the strength that comes from You. I know that I am in a spiritual battle, but You have equipped me with everything I need to stand firm. Help me to put on the full armor of God each day, so that I may stand strong against the enemy's attacks.

Father, when I feel weak or unprepared, remind me that my strength comes from You. Let me trust in Your power and protection as I face every challenge, knowing that You have already won the victory.

Thank You, Lord, for the armor that protects me and the strength to stand firm. In the mighty and matchless name of Jesus, I pray, Amen.

Prayer 61: God's Promise to Answer My Prayers

Scripture:

"Call to Me, and I will answer you, and show you great and mighty things, which you do not know."

(Jeremiah 33:3 NKJV)

Prayer:

Father, I thank You for the promise that when I call on You, You will answer. Today, I come before You with my needs, my concerns, and my heart's desires, knowing that You hear me. I trust that You will show me great and mighty things that I cannot even imagine.

Lord, when I feel like my prayers are unanswered, remind me that Your timing is perfect. Help me to trust in Your wisdom and to wait patiently for Your response, knowing that You are always working for my good.

Thank You, Lord, for hearing and answering my prayers. In the mighty and matchless name of Jesus, I pray, Amen.

Prayer 62: Walking in God's Light

Scripture:

"Your word is a lamp to my feet and a light to my path."
(Psalm 119:105 NKJV)

Prayer:

Lord, I thank You for Your Word, which is the light that guides my steps. When I am unsure of which way to go, I trust that Your Word will lead me on the right path. Help me to seek Your guidance in all things, knowing that You will never lead me astray.

Father, when I feel lost or confused, remind me to turn to Your Word. Let it be the lamp that lights my way, bringing clarity and direction to my life.

Thank You, Lord, for the light of Your Word. In the mighty and matchless name of Jesus, I pray, Amen.

Prayer 63: God's Unfailing Love

Scripture:

"But the mercy of the Lord is from everlasting to everlasting on those who fear Him, and His righteousness to children's children."

(Psalm 103:17 NKJV)

Prayer:

Father, I thank You for Your unfailing love and mercy. Your love endures from generation to generation, and I am so grateful to be a recipient of it. Help me to live in awe of Your mercy and to pass down the knowledge of Your love to my children and those around me.

Lord, when I feel undeserving of Your love, remind me that Your mercy is everlasting. Let me walk confidently in the truth that Your love for me is eternal and never-ending.

Thank You, Lord, for Your enduring love and mercy. In the mighty and matchless name of Jesus, I pray, Amen.

Prayer 64: God's Strength in Trials

Scripture:

"My brethren, count it all joy when you fall into various trials, knowing that the testing of your faith produces patience."

(James 1:2-3 NKJV)

Prayer:

Lord, I thank You for the trials that shape my character and strengthen my faith. It's not always easy to face difficulties, but I trust that You are using them to grow patience in me. Help me to embrace these seasons, knowing that You are working all things for my good.

Father, when I feel discouraged by the challenges I face, remind me that they are temporary and that You are using them to refine me. Let me find joy in the midst of trials, trusting that they are producing something beautiful in me.

Thank You, Lord, for the strength to endure trials and the patience that comes from them. In the mighty and matchless name of Jesus, I pray, Amen.

Prayer 65: Trusting in God's Goodness

Scripture:

"Oh, taste and see that the Lord is good; blessed is the man who trusts in Him!"

(Psalm 34:8 NKJV)

Prayer:

Father, I thank You for Your goodness. I have tasted and seen that You are good, and my heart is filled with gratitude. Help me to trust in You more each day, knowing that those who trust in You are truly blessed.

Lord, when I am tempted to doubt Your goodness, remind me of all the ways You have provided for me and shown me love. Let my trust in You grow stronger, and let me share the goodness of Your love with others.

Thank You, Lord, for being so good to me. In the mighty and matchless name of Jesus, I pray, Amen.

Prayer 66: God's Faithfulness in Answering Prayers

Scripture:

"Before they call, I will answer; and while they are still speaking, I will hear."

(Isaiah 65:24 NKJV)

Prayer:

Lord, I thank You for Your faithfulness in hearing and answering my prayers. Even before I call out to You, You are already working on my behalf. I am comforted by the knowledge that You hear me and respond with love and wisdom.

Father, when I am waiting for answers, remind me that You are always listening. Help me to be patient, trusting that You are already at work, even when I cannot see it. Let me rest in Your faithfulness and the assurance that You are always near.

Thank You, Lord, for hearing my prayers before I even speak. In the mighty and matchless name of Jesus, I pray, Amen.

Prayer 67: God's Compassion and Grace

Scripture:

"The Lord is gracious and full of compassion, slow to anger and great in mercy."

(Psalm 145:8 NKJV)

Prayer:

Father, I thank You for Your compassion and grace. You are slow to anger and rich in mercy, always extending kindness to me. Help me to live with that same spirit of compassion toward others, reflecting the love and mercy that You have shown me.

Lord, when I am quick to judge or slow to forgive, remind me of Your grace. Let Your compassion fill my heart so that I may extend grace and mercy to those around me, just as You have done for me.

Thank You, Lord, for Your endless compassion and grace. In the mighty and matchless name of Jesus, I pray, Amen.

Prayer 68: Walking in the Light of God

Scripture:

"For you were once darkness, but now you are light in the Lord. Walk as children of light."

(Ephesians 5:8 NKJV)

Prayer:

Lord, I thank You for bringing me out of darkness and into Your marvelous light. I am no longer bound by the darkness of sin and shame because I now walk in the light of Christ. Help me to live each day as a child of the light, reflecting Your truth and love.

Father, when I am tempted to return to old ways or when the darkness tries to creep in, remind me that I am called to walk in the light. Let me shine brightly for You, pointing others toward the hope that is found in You alone.

Thank You, Lord, for making me a child of light. In the mighty and matchless name of Jesus, I pray, Amen.

Prayer 69: God's Power to Deliver

Scripture:

"And call upon Me in the day of trouble; I will deliver you, and you shall glorify Me."

(Psalm 50:15 NKJV)

Prayer:

Father, I thank You for Your promise to deliver me in times of trouble. When I face challenges or difficulties, I can call on You, and You will come to my aid. I place my trust in Your power to rescue me and bring me through every trial.

Lord, when I am overwhelmed by life's struggles, remind me that You are my deliverer. I will glorify You for the ways You have brought me through, and I trust that You will continue to deliver me from every storm.

Thank You, Lord, for being my deliverer in times of trouble. In the mighty and matchless name of Jesus, I pray, Amen.

Prayer 70: God's Faithfulness to Fulfill His Promises

Scripture:

"He who calls you is faithful, who also will do it."
(1 Thessalonians 5:24 NKJV)

Prayer:

Lord, I thank You for being faithful to fulfill every promise. You have called me, and I trust that You will complete the good work You have begun in me. Help me to hold fast to Your promises, knowing that You will do exactly what You have said.

Father, when I doubt or when I grow impatient, remind me of Your faithfulness. Let me stand firm in the truth that You are always working, even when I cannot see it. I know that You will accomplish all that You have spoken over my life.

Thank You, Lord, for Your unwavering faithfulness. In the mighty and matchless name of Jesus, I pray, Amen.

Prayer 71: Trusting God's Plans for My Life

Scripture:

"For I know the thoughts that I think toward you, says the Lord, thoughts of peace and not of evil, to give you a future and a hope."

(Jeremiah 29:11 NKJV)

Prayer:

Father, I thank You for the plans You have for my life. You know every detail of my future, and I trust that Your plans are full of hope and peace. Help me to surrender my own plans and desires, trusting that what You have in store for me is far greater than anything I could imagine.

Lord, when I am anxious about the future or unsure of what lies ahead, remind me that You are already there. Let me walk in confidence, knowing that You are guiding my steps toward the future You have prepared for me.

Thank You, Lord, for the hope and future You have promised me. In the mighty and matchless name of Jesus, I pray, Amen.

Prayer 72: God's Comfort in Times of Sorrow

Scripture:

"Blessed are those who mourn, for they shall be comforted."
(Matthew 5:4 NKJV)

Prayer:

Lord, I thank You for the comfort You provide in times of sorrow. You see my pain, and You are near to me when I mourn. I place my grief in Your hands today, trusting that You will bring healing and comfort to my heart.

Father, when I feel overwhelmed by loss or sadness, remind me of Your promise to comfort me. Let me feel Your presence close to me, bringing peace to my spirit and strength to carry on.

Thank You, Lord, for being my comforter in times of sorrow. In the mighty and matchless name of Jesus, I pray, Amen.

Prayer 73: God's Wisdom in Every Situation

Scripture:

"If any of you lacks wisdom, let him ask of God, who gives to all liberally and without reproach, and it will be given to him."

(James 1:5 NKJV)

Prayer:

Father, I thank You for the wisdom You provide so freely. Whenever I face situations where I don't know what to do, I can come to You and ask for wisdom, and You will generously give it. Today, I ask for Your wisdom to guide me in every decision, big or small.

Lord, when I feel uncertain or confused, remind me that You are the source of all wisdom. Let Your Spirit lead me, helping me to make choices that honor You and align with Your will.

Thank You, Lord, for the wisdom You provide. In the mighty and matchless name of Jesus, I pray, Amen.

Prayer 74: God's Provision in Every Season

Scripture:

"But my God shall supply all your need according to His riches in glory by Christ Jesus."

(Philippians 4:19 NKJV)

Prayer:

Father, I thank You for being my provider. You know exactly what I need before I even ask, and I trust that You will supply all my needs according to Your riches in glory. Help me to rely on Your provision in every season, whether in abundance or in lack.

Lord, when I feel anxious about my needs, remind me of Your faithfulness to provide. Let me trust in Your timing and Your resources, knowing that You never fail to take care of me.

Thank You, Lord, for meeting every need in my life. In the mighty and matchless name of Jesus, I pray, Amen.

Prayer 75: God's Protection Over My Life

Scripture:

"The Lord shall preserve you from all evil; He shall preserve your soul. The Lord shall preserve your going out and your coming in from this time forth, and even forevermore."
(Psalm 121:7-8 NKJV)

Prayer:

Lord, I thank You for Your constant protection over my life. You are my shield and my fortress, guarding me from all evil. I trust in Your promise to preserve my going out and coming in, knowing that You are with me in every step I take.

Father, when I feel unsafe or vulnerable, remind me of Your protective hand. Let me rest in the assurance that You are watching over me, both now and forevermore.

Thank You, Lord, for being my protector. In the mighty and matchless name of Jesus, I pray, Amen.

Prayer 76: God's Peace in My Heart

Scripture:

"And let the peace of God rule in your hearts, to which also you were called in one body; and be thankful."
                                        (Colossians 3:15 NKJV)

Prayer:

Father, I thank You for the peace that comes from You. Today, I choose to let Your peace rule in my heart, pushing aside any anxiety, fear, or worry. Help me to live in that peace, always remembering to be thankful for Your constant presence in my life.

Lord, when stress or chaos surrounds me, remind me to seek Your peace. Let Your peace be the ruler of my heart, guiding my thoughts and actions with calm and assurance.

Thank You, Lord, for the peace that guards my heart. In the mighty and matchless name of Jesus, I pray, Amen.

Prayer 77: God's Compassion Toward Me

Scripture:

"The Lord is good to all, and His tender mercies are over all His works."

(Psalm 145:9 NKJV)

Prayer:

Father, I thank You for Your tender mercy and compassion toward me. You are good to all, and Your mercy is over all Your creation. Help me to rest in the knowledge of Your love, knowing that Your kindness is always extended toward me.

Lord, when I feel undeserving of Your love, remind me of Your great mercy. Let me live each day knowing that I am surrounded by Your tender care, and help me to extend that same compassion to others.

Thank You, Lord, for Your goodness and mercy. In the mighty and matchless name of Jesus, I pray, Amen.

Prayer 78: Strength in Times of Waiting

Scripture:

"But those who wait on the Lord shall renew their strength; they shall mount up with wings like eagles, they shall run and not be weary, they shall walk and not faint."
(Isaiah 40:31 NKJV)

Prayer:

Lord, I thank You for the strength that comes from waiting on You. Sometimes, waiting can feel difficult, but I trust that You are renewing my strength in the process. Help me to wait with patience and faith, knowing that You are working in the unseen.

Father, when I feel weary or tempted to rush ahead, remind me that Your timing is perfect. Let me find rest in You, trusting that You will lift me up and give me the strength to soar.

Thank You, Lord, for renewing my strength as I wait on You. In the mighty and matchless name of Jesus, I pray, Amen.

Prayer 79: God's Guidance in My Life

Scripture:

"Your ears shall hear a word behind you, saying, 'This is the way, walk in it,' whenever you turn to the right hand or whenever you turn to the left."

(Isaiah 30:21 NKJV)

Prayer:

Father, I thank You for guiding me in every step I take. You promise that I will hear Your voice directing me in the way I should go, and I trust that You will lead me on the right path. Help me to listen closely to Your voice, seeking Your direction in all things.

Lord, when I feel unsure of which way to go, remind me that You are my guide. Let me trust in Your wisdom and follow Your leading, knowing that You are always directing my steps.

Thank You, Lord, for being my faithful guide. In the mighty and matchless name of Jesus, I pray, Amen.

Prayer 80: Walking in God's Love

Scripture:

"Beloved, if God so loved us, we also ought to love one another."

(1 John 4:11 NKJV)

Prayer:

Lord, I thank You for the incredible love You have shown me. Because You first loved me, I can now love others with that same love. Help me to walk in love each day, showing kindness, grace, and compassion to those around me.

Father, when I struggle to love, remind me of the depth of Your love for me. Let Your love flow through me, allowing me to love even those who are difficult to love. Let my life be a reflection of Your love to the world.

Thank You, Lord, for teaching me to walk in love. In the mighty and matchless name of Jesus, I pray, Amen.

Prayer 81: Trusting God's Promise of Protection

Scripture:

"The angel of the Lord encamps all around those who fear Him, and delivers them."

(Psalm 34:7 NKJV)

Prayer:

Father, I thank You for the protection You provide. Your Word promises that Your angels encamp around those who fear You, and I trust that You are always watching over me. I place my life in Your hands, knowing that You are my deliverer.

Lord, when I feel afraid or threatened, remind me that You have placed a hedge of protection around me. Let me walk in confidence, knowing that You are my shield and my defender.

Thank You, Lord, for Your constant protection. In the mighty and matchless name of Jesus, I pray, Amen.

Prayer 82: God's Unfailing Word

Scripture:

"Heaven and earth will pass away, but My words will by no means pass away."

(Matthew 24:35 NKJV)

Prayer:

Father, I thank You for the power of Your Word. Your promises are eternal, and Your Word will never fade. Help me to build my life on the foundation of Your truth, knowing that it is unchanging and everlasting.

Lord, when I face challenges or uncertainties, remind me of the power of Your Word. Let me trust in Your promises and hold fast to the truth, knowing that Your Word stands forever.

Thank You, Lord, for the enduring power of Your Word. In the mighty and matchless name of Jesus, I pray, Amen.

Prayer 83: God's Power in My Life

Scripture:

"Now to Him who is able to do exceedingly abundantly above all that we ask or think, according to the power that works in us."

(Ephesians 3:20 NKJV)

Prayer:

Lord, I thank You for the power that is at work within me through Your Holy Spirit. You are able to do far more than I could ever ask or imagine, and I trust that Your power is at work in my life. Help me to walk in the confidence of that power, knowing that You are always with me.

Father, when I face challenges that seem too big, remind me that Your power is greater. Let me rely on Your strength and not my own, trusting that You are able to accomplish more than I could ever dream.

Thank You, Lord, for Your mighty power at work in me. In the mighty and matchless name of Jesus, I pray, Amen.

Prayer 84: God's Mercy in My Life

Scripture:

"Through the Lord's mercies we are not consumed, because His compassions fail not. They are new every morning; great is Your faithfulness."

(Lamentations 3:22-23 NKJV)

Prayer:

Father, I thank You for Your mercies that are new every morning. It is because of Your compassion that I am not consumed by life's troubles. Help me to wake up each day with a grateful heart, knowing that Your mercy and faithfulness never fail.

Lord, when I feel burdened by guilt or shame, remind me of Your mercy. Let me live in the freedom of Your forgiveness, trusting that Your grace is more than enough to cover my sins.

Thank You, Lord, for Your unfailing mercy and great faithfulness. In the mighty and matchless name of Jesus, I pray, Amen.

Prayer 85: God's Everlasting Covenant

Scripture:

"This is the covenant that I will make with them after those days, says the Lord: I will put My laws into their hearts, and in their minds I will write them."

(Hebrews 10:16 NKJV)

Prayer:

Father, I thank You for the new covenant You have made with me through Jesus. You have placed Your laws in my heart and mind, transforming me from the inside out. Help me to live in accordance with Your Word, allowing it to guide my thoughts and actions.

Lord, when I struggle to obey or follow Your ways, remind me of the promise of this covenant. Fill me with Your Spirit and empower me to live a life that reflects Your love and truth.

Thank You, Lord, for the everlasting covenant You have established with me. In the mighty and matchless name of Jesus, I pray, Amen.

Prayer 86: God's Guidance in Every Step

Scripture:

"The steps of a good man are ordered by the Lord, and He delights in his way."

(Psalm 37:23 NKJV)

Prayer:

Father, I thank You for ordering my steps. I trust that You are directing my path and guiding me in the way I should go. Help me to be attentive to Your leading, knowing that You delight in the journey of my life.

Lord, when I feel unsure of the next step to take, remind me to seek Your guidance. Let me walk in faith, trusting that You are guiding me toward what is best for me.

Thank You, Lord, for directing my steps and delighting in my journey. In the mighty and matchless name of Jesus, I pray, Amen.

Prayer 87: God's Peace in My Soul

Scripture:

"Peace I leave with you, My peace I give to you; not as the world gives do I give to you. Let not your heart be troubled, neither let it be afraid."

(John 14:27 NKJV)

Prayer:

Lord, I thank You for the gift of peace that Jesus provides. In a world full of chaos and uncertainty, Your peace is a refuge for my soul. Help me to embrace that peace today, letting it calm my heart and mind.

Father, when anxiety or fear tries to take hold of me, remind me of the peace You have given. Let me rest in Your assurance, knowing that I do not have to be troubled or afraid because You are always with me.

Thank You, Lord, for the peace that surpasses all understanding. In the mighty and matchless name of Jesus, I pray, Amen.

Prayer 88: God's Abundant Grace

Scripture:

"And God is able to make all grace abound toward you, that you, always having all sufficiency in all things, may have an abundance for every good work."

(2 Corinthians 9:8 NKJV)

Prayer:

Father, I thank You for the abundance of Your grace. Your grace is sufficient for every situation I face, and I trust that You will provide everything I need. Help me to recognize and rely on Your grace in every aspect of my life.

Lord, when I feel inadequate or overwhelmed, remind me that Your grace is enough. Let me walk in the confidence of Your sufficiency, knowing that You have equipped me for every good work You have called me to do.

Thank You, Lord, for Your abundant grace in my life. In the mighty and matchless name of Jesus, I pray, Amen.

Prayer 89: God's Faithfulness in My Journey

Scripture:

"The Lord your God, who goes before you, will fight for you, according to all He did for you in Egypt before your eyes."

(Deuteronomy 1:30 NKJV)

Prayer:

Father, I thank You for going before me in every battle. You are always at work, preparing the way and fighting for me. Help me to trust in Your faithfulness as I navigate the journey of life, knowing that You have already won the victory.

Lord, when I face challenges or feel overwhelmed, remind me of all the times You have come through for me in the past. Let my faith be strengthened as I remember Your goodness and faithfulness.

Thank You, Lord, for being my warrior and guide. In the mighty and matchless name of Jesus, I pray, Amen.

Prayer 90: The Blessing of Obedience

Scripture:

"If you are willing and obedient, you shall eat the good of the land."

(Isaiah 1:19 NKJV)

Prayer:

Father, I thank You for the blessing that comes from obedience. When I choose to follow Your ways and trust in Your guidance, I experience the goodness of Your promises. Help me to be willing and obedient, seeking to honor You in all that I do.

Lord, when I am tempted to go my own way, remind me of the blessings that come from walking in Your truth. Let my heart desire to please You, knowing that You have my best interests at heart.

Thank You, Lord, for the joy of obedience and the blessings that follow. In the mighty and matchless name of Jesus, I pray, Amen.

Prayer 91: God's Presence in My Life

Scripture:

"For I know the plans I have for you, says the Lord, plans to prosper you and not to harm you, plans to give you hope and a future."

(Jeremiah 29:11 NKJV)

Prayer:

Lord, I thank You for the beautiful plans You have for my life. You have a purpose for me, and I trust that You are leading me toward a hopeful future. Help me to embrace Your plans, even when I cannot see the full picture.

Father, when I feel lost or uncertain, remind me that Your presence is always with me. Let me find comfort in the knowledge that You are guiding me toward the future You have prepared.

Thank You, Lord, for the hope and future You promise. In the mighty and matchless name of Jesus, I pray, Amen.

Prayer 92: God's Healing in My Life

Scripture:

"He heals the brokenhearted and binds up their wounds."
(Psalm 147:3 NKJV)

Prayer:

Father, I thank You for being my healer. You see my pain and brokenness, and I trust that You are able to mend my heart and restore my soul. Help me to bring my wounds to You, knowing that You care deeply for me.

Lord, when I feel overwhelmed by grief or hurt, remind me that You are with me to heal. Let Your healing touch bring comfort and restoration to every area of my life.

Thank You, Lord, for Your healing power and compassion. In the mighty and matchless name of Jesus, I pray, Amen.

Prayer 93: God's Strength in My Faith

Scripture:

"I can do all things through Christ who strengthens me."
(Philippians 4:13 NKJV)

Prayer:

Lord, I thank You for the strength You provide. In moments when I feel weak or inadequate, I remember that I can do all things through Christ who strengthens me. Help me to rely on Your power, trusting that You will equip me for every task ahead.

Father, when I face challenges that seem impossible, remind me that I am not alone. Let me lean on Your strength and walk in confidence, knowing that You are with me every step of the way.

Thank You, Lord, for empowering me through Christ. In the mighty and matchless name of Jesus, I pray, Amen.

Prayer 94: God's Love in My Relationships

Scripture:

"Above all things have fervent love for one another, for 'love will cover a multitude of sins.'
(1 Peter 4:8 NKJV)

Prayer:

Father, I thank You for the love You have poured into my heart. Help me to extend that love to those around me, especially in my relationships. Teach me to love others fervently, understanding that love can heal and restore even the deepest wounds.

Lord, when conflicts arise or when I feel frustrated with others, remind me of Your command to love. Let my heart be filled with compassion, and let my love cover any offenses, reflecting Your grace and mercy.

Thank You, Lord, for the power of love in my life. In the mighty and matchless name of Jesus, I pray, Amen.

Prayer 95: God's Light Guiding My Way

Scripture:

"For with You is the fountain of life; in Your light we see light."

(Psalm 36:9 NKJV)

Prayer:

Lord, I thank You for being the fountain of life and the source of all light. Your light illuminates my path and reveals the way I should go. Help me to walk in Your light, seeking Your guidance in every decision I make.

Father, when darkness tries to overshadow my life, remind me to turn to You. Let Your light shine brightly in my heart, guiding me through the challenges I face.

Thank You, Lord, for being my light and guiding my way. In the mighty and matchless name of Jesus, I pray, Amen.

Prayer 96: God's Joy in My Life

Scripture:

"You have turned for me my mourning into dancing; You have put off my sackcloth and clothed me with gladness."
(Psalm 30:11 NKJV)

Prayer:

Father, I thank You for the joy that comes from You. You have the power to transform my sorrow into joy, and I trust that You are working in my life to bring about that change. Help me to embrace Your joy, even in the midst of challenges.

Lord, when I feel weighed down by life's struggles, remind me of the joy that comes from knowing You. Let Your gladness fill my heart and overflow into every area of my life.

Thank You, Lord, for turning my mourning into dancing. In the mighty and matchless name of Jesus, I pray, Amen.

Prayer 97: God's Faithfulness Through Trials

Scripture:

"Many are the afflictions of the righteous, but the Lord delivers him out of them all."

(Psalm 34:19 NKJV)

Prayer:

Lord, I thank You for Your promise of deliverance. Although I may face afflictions and trials, I trust that You are with me in every situation. Help me to lean on You during difficult times, knowing that You are faithful to deliver me.

Father, when I feel overwhelmed by challenges, remind me of Your faithfulness. Let me rest in the assurance that You will rescue me and bring me through every storm I encounter.

Thank You, Lord, for Your deliverance in my life. In the mighty and matchless name of Jesus, I pray, Amen.

Prayer 98: God's Comfort in Times of Need

Scripture:

"Blessed are those who mourn, for they shall be comforted."
(Matthew 5:4 NKJV)

Prayer:

Father, I thank You for the comfort You provide to those who mourn. You see my pain and my heartache, and I trust that You are near to comfort me. Help me to lean on You in my times of sorrow, knowing that You will provide the healing I need.

Lord, when I feel lost in my grief, remind me that You are with me to comfort and guide me. Let Your presence surround me, bringing peace and hope to my weary soul.

Thank You, Lord, for being my comforter in times of need. In the mighty and matchless name of Jesus, I pray, Amen.

Prayer 99: God's Promise of New Beginnings

Scripture:

"Therefore, if anyone is in Christ, he is a new creation; old things have passed away; behold, all things have become new."

(2 Corinthians 5:17 NKJV)

Prayer:

Lord, I thank You for the new life I have in Christ. Because of Him, I am a new creation, and my past no longer defines me. Help me to embrace this new beginning and to live in the freedom and hope that comes with it.

Father, when I feel weighed down by my past mistakes, remind me that I am made new in You. Let me walk forward in faith, knowing that You have a fresh start waiting for me every day.

Thank You, Lord, for the promise of new beginnings. In the mighty and matchless name of Jesus, I pray, Amen.

Prayer 100: God's Light in the Darkness

Scripture:

"The people who walked in darkness have seen a great light; those who dwelt in the land of the shadow of death, upon them a light has shined."

(Isaiah 9:2 NKJV)

Prayer:

Father, I thank You for the light of Christ that shines in my darkness. In times when I feel lost or surrounded by despair, I am reminded that Your light brings hope and clarity. Help me to seek Your light in every situation, trusting that it will guide me.

Lord, when I encounter darkness in my life, remind me that Your light is greater. Let me shine that light to others, sharing the hope that comes from knowing You.

Thank You, Lord, for being the light in my life. In the mighty and matchless name of Jesus, I pray, Amen.

Prayer 101: God's Presence in My Life

Scripture:

"For He Himself has said, 'I will never leave you nor forsake you.'"

(Hebrews 13:5 NKJV)

Prayer:

Father, I thank You for the promise of Your constant presence in my life. You have assured me that You will never leave me or forsake me. Help me to remember this truth in every situation, knowing that I am never alone.

Lord, when I feel isolated or abandoned, remind me that You are always by my side. Let Your presence bring me comfort and strength as I navigate through life's challenges.

Thank You, Lord, for Your unfailing presence. In the mighty and matchless name of Jesus, I pray, Amen.

Prayer 102: God's Wisdom in My Choices

Scripture:

"The Lord gives wisdom; from His mouth come knowledge and understanding."

(Proverbs 2:6 NKJV)

Prayer:

Father, I thank You for the gift of wisdom that comes from You. In a world full of choices and distractions, I seek Your guidance in every decision I make. Help me to listen to Your voice and to seek Your wisdom above all else.

Lord, when I am faced with difficult choices, remind me to turn to You first. Let Your wisdom guide my thoughts and actions, leading me toward what is right and pleasing to You.

Thank You, Lord, for being my source of wisdom. In the mighty and matchless name of Jesus, I pray, Amen.

Prayer 103: God's Faithfulness in My Life

Scripture:

"Jesus Christ is the same yesterday, today, and forever."
(Hebrews 13:8 NKJV)

Prayer:

Lord, I thank You for Your unwavering faithfulness. You are the same yesterday, today, and forever, and I can always count on You. Help me to remember Your faithfulness in my life, especially during times of doubt or uncertainty.

Father, when I feel shaken by the circumstances around me, remind me that You remain constant. Let me hold fast to Your promises and trust in Your character, knowing that You will never change.

Thank You, Lord, for Your everlasting faithfulness. In the mighty and matchless name of Jesus, I pray, Amen.

Prayer 104: God's Compassion for the Brokenhearted

Scripture:

"The Lord is near to those who have a broken heart, and saves such as have a contrite spirit."
(Psalm 34:18 NKJV)

Prayer:

Father, I thank You for Your compassion toward those who are hurting. You are near to the brokenhearted, and I trust that You understand my pain. Help me to bring my brokenness to You, knowing that You can heal and restore my heart.

Lord, when I feel crushed by grief or loss, remind me of Your comforting presence. Let me feel Your arms around me, bringing me the peace and hope I need to heal.

Thank You, Lord, for being close to me in my pain. In the mighty and matchless name of Jesus, I pray, Amen.

Prayer 105: God's Peace Amidst Chaos

Scripture:

"And the peace of God, which surpasses all understanding, will guard your hearts and minds through Christ Jesus."
(Philippians 4:7 NKJV)

Prayer:

Lord, I thank You for the peace that comes from knowing You. Your peace surpasses all understanding, guarding my heart and mind in every circumstance. Help me to seek that peace and to rest in Your presence, especially when chaos surrounds me.

Father, when anxiety tries to creep in, remind me to turn my worries into prayers. Let Your peace fill my heart, bringing calm in the storm and assurance that You are in control.

Thank You, Lord, for the peace that guards my heart. In the mighty and matchless name of Jesus, I pray, Amen.

Prayer 106: God's Comfort in Trials

Scripture:

"Blessed be the God and Father of our Lord Jesus Christ, the Father of mercies and God of all comfort, who comforts us in all our tribulation."

(2 Corinthians 1:3-4 NKJV)

Prayer:

Father, I thank You for being the God of all comfort. In times of trial and hardship, You are there to provide solace and peace. Help me to lean on You during difficult times, trusting that You will bring me comfort and healing.

Lord, when I feel overwhelmed by my struggles, remind me that You are the Father of mercies. Let me find refuge in Your presence, knowing that You understand my pain and will provide the comfort I need.

Thank You, Lord, for Your unwavering comfort in my life. In the mighty and matchless name of Jesus, I pray, Amen.

Prayer 107: God's Promise of Restoration

Scripture:

"So I will restore to you the years that the swarming locust has eaten."

(Joel 2:25 NKJV)

Prayer:

Lord, I thank You for Your promise of restoration. No matter what I have lost or what has been taken from me, I trust that You are able to restore it. Help me to believe in Your ability to bring beauty from ashes and to redeem my past.

Father, when I feel discouraged about what has been lost, remind me of Your faithfulness. Let me look forward with hope, knowing that You can and will restore what has been damaged in my life.

Thank You, Lord, for the promise of restoration. In the mighty and matchless name of Jesus, I pray, Amen.

Prayer 108: God's Love is Unconditional

Scripture:

"For I am persuaded that neither death nor life, nor angels nor principalities, nor powers, nor things present, nor things to come, nor height nor depth, nor any other created thing, shall be able to separate us from the love of God which is in Christ Jesus our Lord."
(Romans 8:38-39 NKJV)

Prayer:

Father, I thank You for Your unconditional love. There is nothing in this world that can separate me from Your love, and I am so grateful for that assurance. Help me to rest in the truth that I am loved beyond measure, regardless of my circumstances.

Lord, when I feel unworthy or distant, remind me of the depth of Your love. Let me hold onto that truth and share it with others, knowing that Your love can transform hearts and lives.

Thank You, Lord, for Your unwavering love. In the mighty and matchless name of Jesus, I pray, Amen.

Prayer 109: God's Faithfulness in All Things

Scripture:

"The steadfast love of the Lord never ceases; His mercies never come to an end; they are new every morning; great is Your faithfulness."

(Lamentations 3:22-23 NKJV)

Prayer:

Lord, I thank You for Your steadfast love and faithfulness. Each day is a new opportunity to experience Your mercies, and I am so grateful for that. Help me to wake up with a heart full of gratitude, ready to embrace the new day You have given me.

Father, when I feel discouraged or overwhelmed, remind me of Your faithfulness. Let me trust in Your goodness and walk in the confidence that You are with me every step of the way.

Thank You, Lord, for Your endless faithfulness. In the mighty and matchless name of Jesus, I pray, Amen.

Prayer 110: God's Strength in My Journey

Scripture:

"The Lord is my strength and song, and He has become my salvation."

(Psalm 118:14 NKJV)

Prayer:

Father, I thank You for being my strength and my song. You are the source of my joy and the one who carries me through every trial. Help me to rely on Your strength as I navigate my journey, trusting that You will lead me to victory.

Lord, when I feel weak or defeated, remind me that You are my salvation. Let my heart sing praises to You, knowing that You are my refuge and my strength in every situation.

Thank You, Lord, for being my strength and my song. In the mighty and matchless name of Jesus, I pray, Amen.

Prayer 111: God's Guidance Through the Unknown

Scripture:

"I will instruct you and teach you in the way you should go; I will guide you with My eye."

(Psalm 32:8 NKJV)

Prayer:

Father, I thank You for Your promise to instruct and guide me. Even when I find myself in unknown territory, I trust that You are leading me every step of the way. Help me to be attentive to Your voice and sensitive to Your guidance.

Lord, when I feel confused or unsure of the path ahead, remind me that You are watching over me and will provide the direction I need. Let me walk confidently, knowing that Your eye is upon me.

Thank You, Lord, for guiding me in every situation. In the mighty and matchless name of Jesus, I pray, Amen.

Prayer 112: God's Promise of Hope

Scripture:

"For I know the thoughts that I think toward you, says the Lord, thoughts of peace and not of evil, to give you a future and a hope."

(Jeremiah 29:11 NKJV)

Prayer:

Lord, I thank You for the hope You have promised me. Your plans for my life are filled with peace and a bright future, and I choose to trust in that today. Help me to hold onto that hope, even when circumstances seem difficult or uncertain.

Father, when I feel despair creeping in, remind me of Your good plans for my life. Let my heart be filled with hope, knowing that You are always working for my good.

Thank You, Lord, for the hope and future You have for me. In the mighty and matchless name of Jesus, I pray, Amen.

Prayer 113: God's Peace in the Storm

Scripture:

"He calms the storm, so that its waves are still."
(Psalm 107:29 NKJV)

Prayer:

Father, I thank You for the power You have over every storm in my life. You have the ability to calm the raging waves and bring peace in the midst of chaos. Help me to trust in Your power when the storms of life seem overwhelming.

Lord, when I am caught in turmoil or fear, remind me to look to You for peace. Let me find comfort in the knowledge that You are in control and can bring stillness to my heart.

Thank You, Lord, for calming the storms in my life. In the mighty and matchless name of Jesus, I pray, Amen.

Prayer 114: God's Restoration in My Life

Scripture:

"And I will restore to you the years that the swarming locust has eaten."

(Joel 2:25 NKJV)

Prayer:

Lord, I thank You for Your promise of restoration. No matter what I have lost or what has been taken from me, I trust that You can restore it. Help me to believe in Your power to heal and to bring back the joy I once had.

Father, when I reflect on my past losses, remind me that You are a God of restoration. Let me look forward with hope, knowing that You can turn my mourning into dancing and my despair into joy.

Thank You, Lord, for the restoration You promise. In the mighty and matchless name of Jesus, I pray, Amen.

Prayer 115: God's Comfort in Grief

Scripture:

"Blessed are those who mourn, for they shall be comforted."
(Matthew 5:4 NKJV)

Prayer:

Father, I thank You for the comfort You provide to those who grieve. You see my pain, and You are close to me in my sorrow. Help me to lean on You during these difficult times, trusting that You will bring healing to my heart.

Lord, when I feel overwhelmed by grief, remind me of Your promise to comfort me. Let me feel Your loving presence surrounding me, bringing peace and hope as I navigate through my pain.

Thank You, Lord, for being my comforter in times of sorrow. In the mighty and matchless name of Jesus, I pray, Amen.

Prayer 116: God's Strength in My Journey

Scripture:

"But those who wait on the Lord shall renew their strength; they shall mount up with wings like eagles."
(Isaiah 40:31 NKJV)

Prayer:

Lord, I thank You for the strength You give to those who wait on You. I choose to wait patiently, trusting that You are renewing my strength and preparing me for what lies ahead. Help me to embrace the waiting period, knowing that You are working in my life.

Father, when I feel weary or tempted to rush ahead, remind me that Your timing is perfect. Let me soar above my challenges, empowered by Your strength and grace.

Thank You, Lord, for renewing my strength as I wait on You. In the mighty and matchless name of Jesus, I pray, Amen.

Prayer 117: God's Wisdom for the Future

Scripture:

"The heart of man plans his way, but the Lord establishes his steps."

(Proverbs 16:9 ESV)

Prayer:

Father, I thank You for establishing my steps. I may have my plans and dreams, but I trust that You have a purpose for my life that goes beyond my understanding. Help me to submit my plans to You and seek Your guidance in every decision I make.

Lord, when my plans change or don't go as expected, remind me that You are in control. Let me walk confidently, knowing that You are directing my steps toward a future filled with hope.

Thank You, Lord, for guiding my path and establishing my steps. In the mighty and matchless name of Jesus, I pray, Amen.

Prayer 118: God's Healing for My Soul

Scripture:

"He heals the brokenhearted and binds up their wounds."
(Psalm 147:3 NKJV)

Prayer:

Lord, I thank You for being my healer. You see the wounds of my heart and the brokenness I carry, and I trust that You are able to mend and restore. Help me to bring my pain to You, knowing that You are the One who can heal me.

Father, when I feel overwhelmed by grief or hurt, remind me that You are near to the brokenhearted. Let Your healing touch bring comfort and restoration to my soul.

Thank You, Lord, for Your healing power. In the mighty and matchless name of Jesus, I pray, Amen.

Prayer 119: God's Faithfulness in Every Trial

Scripture:

"Consider it pure joy, my brothers and sisters, whenever you face trials of many kinds."

(James 1:2 NIV)

Prayer:

Father, I thank You for the strength to face trials with joy. Though challenges may come my way, I know that they are producing perseverance and faith within me. Help me to see the bigger picture in my struggles, knowing that You are using them for my good.

Lord, when I encounter difficulties, remind me to choose joy and to lean on Your faithfulness. Let me trust that You are refining me through these experiences, making me stronger and more resilient.

Thank You, Lord, for Your faithfulness in every trial I face. In the mighty and matchless name of Jesus, I pray, Amen.

Prayer 120: God's Blessing Over My Life

Scripture:

"The Lord bless you and keep you; the Lord make His face shine upon you, and be gracious to you."
(Numbers 6:24-25 NKJV)

Prayer:

Lord, I thank You for Your blessings in my life. Your grace and favor shine upon me, and I trust in Your promises to keep me safe and secure. Help me to recognize and appreciate the blessings You have given me each day.

Father, when I feel overwhelmed by challenges, remind me of Your goodness and grace. Let me walk in confidence, knowing that You are watching over me and blessing my life.

Thank You, Lord, for Your blessings and grace. In the mighty and matchless name of Jesus, I pray, Amen.

Prayer 121: God's Assurance of His Presence

Scripture:

"For I am with you, says the Lord, to save you; for I will make a full end of all the nations to which I have driven you, but I will not make a full end of you. I will chasten you in just measure, and I will not leave you altogether unpunished."

(Jeremiah 30:11 NKJV)

Prayer:

Father, I thank You for Your promise of presence. You are always with me, guiding and protecting me. Even in difficult times, I can trust that You are near. Help me to recognize Your presence in my life and to rely on You in every situation.

Lord, when I feel alone or abandoned, remind me that You are always by my side. Let me find comfort in the knowledge that You are saving and sustaining me through all my trials.

Thank You, Lord, for Your unchanging presence. In the mighty and matchless name of Jesus, I pray, Amen.

Prayer 122: God's Perfect Timing

Scripture:

"He has made everything beautiful in its time. Also, He has put eternity in their hearts, except that no one can find out the work that God does from beginning to end."

(Ecclesiastes 3:11 NKJV)

Prayer:

Lord, I thank You for Your perfect timing. I trust that You are working all things according to Your plan, even when I cannot see it. Help me to be patient and to wait on You, knowing that everything happens in Your timing.

Father, when I feel impatient or frustrated, remind me that Your timing is always perfect. Let me find peace in the process, trusting that You are crafting something beautiful in my life.

Thank You, Lord, for the beauty of Your timing. In the mighty and matchless name of Jesus, I pray, Amen.

Prayer 123: God's Compassionate Heart

Scripture:

"The Lord is gracious and full of compassion, slow to anger and great in mercy."

(Psalm 145:8 NKJV)

Prayer:

Father, I thank You for Your compassionate heart. Your grace and mercy are abundant, and I am grateful for the love You extend to me daily. Help me to reflect that same compassion to those around me, showing kindness and understanding.

Lord, when I encounter difficult people or situations, remind me of Your mercy. Let my heart be filled with compassion, allowing me to love others as You have loved me.

Thank You, Lord, for Your infinite compassion. In the mighty and matchless name of Jesus, I pray, Amen.

Prayer 124: God's Wisdom in the Trials

Scripture:

"If any of you lacks wisdom, let him ask of God, who gives to all liberally and without reproach, and it will be given to him."

(James 1:5 NKJV)

Prayer:

Lord, I thank You for the gift of wisdom. I ask for Your guidance in every trial I face, trusting that You will provide the understanding I need. Help me to seek You first when making decisions, knowing that You will generously give me wisdom.

Father, when I feel confused or lost, remind me to come to You. Let Your wisdom illuminate my path, leading me in the right direction and helping me to navigate through difficulties.

Thank You, Lord, for Your wisdom that guides me. In the mighty and matchless name of Jesus, I pray, Amen.

Prayer 125: God's Comfort in My Grief

Scripture:

"The Lord is near to those who have a broken heart, and saves such as have a contrite spirit."
                                (Psalm 34:18 NKJV)

Prayer:

Father, I thank You for Your comfort in my times of grief. You are near to me when my heart is broken, and I trust that You will bring healing to my pain. Help me to lean on You for support and solace during these difficult moments.

Lord, when I feel overwhelmed by sorrow, remind me that You understand my heartache. Let Your presence bring me peace and comfort, allowing me to feel Your love surrounding me.

Thank You, Lord, for being my comforter. In the mighty and matchless name of Jesus, I pray, Amen.

Prayer 126: God's Promise of Restoration

Scripture:

"I will restore to you the years that the swarming locust has eaten."

(Joel 2:25 NKJV)

Prayer:

Lord, I thank You for Your promise of restoration. I trust that You can redeem the time that has been lost and bring healing to the areas of my life that have been damaged. Help me to believe in Your power to restore all things.

Father, when I look back at my past and see loss or pain, remind me that You are able to bring beauty from ashes. Let me walk in faith, trusting that You are working to restore and renew my life.

Thank You, Lord, for the gift of restoration. In the mighty and matchless name of Jesus, I pray, Amen.

Prayer 127: God's Faithfulness Through Trials

Scripture:

"Many are the afflictions of the righteous, but the Lord delivers him out of them all."

(Psalm 34:19 NKJV)

Prayer:

Father, I thank You for Your faithfulness in my trials. I know that while I may face afflictions, You are always there to deliver me. Help me to trust in Your promises during difficult times, knowing that You will see me through.

Lord, when I feel overwhelmed by my struggles, remind me of Your past deliverances. Let my faith be strengthened as I remember how You have always been there for me.

Thank You, Lord, for Your faithfulness in every trial. In the mighty and matchless name of Jesus, I pray, Amen.

Prayer 128: God's Light in My Life

Scripture:

"The Lord is my light and my salvation; whom shall I fear? The Lord is the strength of my life; of whom shall I be afraid?"

(Psalm 27:1 NKJV)

Prayer:

Lord, I thank You for being my light and salvation. With You guiding my life, I have nothing to fear. Help me to walk in Your light, trusting in Your strength and protection as I face the uncertainties of life.

Father, when darkness surrounds me or fear tries to creep in, remind me that Your light dispels all shadows. Let me find comfort in knowing that You are always by my side, illuminating my path.

Thank You, Lord, for being my light and salvation. In the mighty and matchless name of Jesus, I pray, Amen.

Prayer 129: God's Love is Unconditional

Scripture:

"But God demonstrates His own love toward us, in that while we were still sinners, Christ died for us."
(Romans 5:8 NKJV)

Prayer:

Father, I thank You for the incredible love You have shown me through Christ. Your love is unconditional, and I am forever grateful that You sacrificed everything for me. Help me to fully grasp the depth of that love and to share it with others.

Lord, when I feel unworthy or distant, remind me that Your love is not based on my performance. Let me rest in the truth that I am loved and accepted just as I am.

Thank You, Lord, for Your unconditional love. In the mighty and matchless name of Jesus, I pray, Amen.

Prayer 130: God's Strength in My Weakness

Scripture:

"But He said to me, 'My grace is sufficient for you, for My strength is made perfect in weakness.'"

(2 Corinthians 12:9 NKJV)

Prayer:

Lord, I thank You for Your grace that is sufficient for every need. In my weakness, I find strength in You. Help me to embrace my limitations, knowing that Your power is made perfect in my frailty.

Father, when I feel overwhelmed or incapable, remind me to lean on Your strength. Let me walk in the assurance that I am strong because You are with me, empowering me to face every challenge.

Thank You, Lord, for Your sufficient grace and strength. In the mighty and matchless name of Jesus, I pray, Amen.

Prayer 131: God's Peace in Times of Trouble

Scripture:

"In the world you will have tribulation; but be of good cheer, I have overcome the world."

(John 16:33 NKJV)

Prayer:

Father, I thank You for the assurance that even in this world, filled with troubles, I can have peace in You. You have overcome the challenges I face, and I choose to rest in that truth. Help me to remain cheerful and hopeful, knowing that You are victorious.

Lord, when tribulation surrounds me, remind me to look to You for strength and comfort. Let Your peace fill my heart, allowing me to face each day with courage and joy.

Thank You, Lord, for the peace that comes from knowing You have overcome the world. In the mighty and matchless name of Jesus, I pray, Amen.

Prayer 132: God's Faithfulness in Every Season

Scripture:

"Jesus Christ is the same yesterday, today, and forever."
(Hebrews 13:8 NKJV)

Prayer:

Lord, I thank You for Your unchanging faithfulness. You remain the same through every season of my life, and I can always count on You. Help me to trust in Your character, knowing that You will never fail me.

Father, when life feels unpredictable, remind me that You are my constant. Let me rest in the assurance that You are with me, guiding and providing every step of the way.

Thank You, Lord, for Your unwavering faithfulness. In the mighty and matchless name of Jesus, I pray, Amen.

Prayer 133: God's Goodness in My Life

Scripture:

"Oh, taste and see that the Lord is good; blessed is the man who trusts in Him."

(Psalm 34:8 NKJV)

Prayer:

Father, I thank You for Your goodness. I have tasted and seen that You are good, and I am grateful for the blessings You pour into my life. Help me to continually trust in You, experiencing the richness of Your goodness every day.

Lord, when I feel discouraged or overwhelmed, remind me of Your goodness. Let me reflect on all the ways You have been faithful, and may that lead me to deeper trust in You.

Thank You, Lord, for Your goodness that never fades. In the mighty and matchless name of Jesus, I pray, Amen.

Prayer 134: God's Call to Love Others

Scripture:

"And you shall love the Lord your God with all your heart, with all your soul, and with all your strength."

(Deuteronomy 6:5 NKJV)

Prayer:

Lord, I thank You for the command to love You with all my heart, soul, and strength. Help me to prioritize my relationship with You above all else, pouring my love into seeking Your will and presence in my life.

Father, as I grow in my love for You, teach me to love others with that same passion. Let me reflect Your love in my interactions and relationships, demonstrating kindness and compassion to everyone I meet.

Thank You, Lord, for the call to love and the strength to do so. In the mighty and matchless name of Jesus, I pray, Amen.

Prayer 135: God's Strength in My Challenges

Scripture:

"But the Lord is faithful, who will establish you and guard you from the evil one."

(2 Thessalonians 3:3 NKJV)

Prayer:

Father, I thank You for Your faithfulness. You establish me in the face of challenges and guard my heart from harm. Help me to trust in Your protection and strength as I navigate through the difficulties of life.

Lord, when I feel vulnerable or threatened, remind me that You are always watching over me. Let me find comfort in knowing that You are my protector and that Your strength is made perfect in my weakness.

Thank You, Lord, for being my faithful guard. In the mighty and matchless name of Jesus, I pray, Amen.

Prayer 136: God's Promise of Hope and Healing

Scripture:

"For I will restore health to you, and your wounds I will heal, says the Lord."

(Jeremiah 30:17 NKJV)

Prayer:

Lord, I thank You for Your promise to restore my health and heal my wounds. I trust in Your ability to bring healing to every area of my life—physically, emotionally, and spiritually. Help me to seek Your healing touch and to walk in faith as I await Your restoration.

Father, when I feel weighed down by pain or heartache, remind me of Your promise. Let me bring my burdens to You, knowing that You care for me and are working to heal and restore.

Thank You, Lord, for Your promise of hope and healing. In the mighty and matchless name of Jesus, I pray, Amen.

Prayer 137: God's Comfort in the Storm

Scripture:

"When you pass through the waters, I will be with you; and through the rivers, they shall not overflow you. When you walk through the fire, you shall not be burned, nor shall the flame scorch you."

(Isaiah 43:2 NKJV)

Prayer:

Father, I thank You for the assurance that You are with me in every storm I face. No matter how overwhelming the waters or how intense the fire, I can trust that You are my protector. Help me to remember Your presence in times of trouble.

Lord, when I feel engulfed by challenges, remind me that I am not alone. Let me lean on You for strength and comfort, trusting that You will see me through every trial.

Thank You, Lord, for being with me in every storm. In the mighty and matchless name of Jesus, I pray, Amen.

Prayer 138: God's Goodness and Mercy

Scripture:

"Surely goodness and mercy shall follow me all the days of my life; and I will dwell in the house of the Lord forever."
(Psalm 23:6 NKJV)

Prayer:

Lord, I thank You for the promise of Your goodness and mercy following me every day. I am grateful for Your faithfulness and the blessings You shower upon me. Help me to recognize and appreciate Your goodness in every aspect of my life.

Father, when I feel discouraged, remind me that Your goodness is always present. Let me dwell in Your house, enjoying the peace and security that comes from being in Your presence.

Thank You, Lord, for Your goodness and mercy that are always with me. In the mighty and matchless name of Jesus, I pray, Amen.

Prayer 139: God's Faithfulness Through Trials

Scripture:

"The Lord is good, a stronghold in the day of trouble; and He knows those who trust in Him."

(Nahum 1:7 NKJV)

Prayer:

Father, I thank You for being my stronghold in times of trouble. You are good and faithful, and I can always rely on You when life gets difficult. Help me to trust You completely, knowing that You are aware of my struggles and will protect me.

Lord, when I feel overwhelmed by challenges, remind me of Your goodness. Let me find refuge in You, confident that You will guide me through every storm.

Thank You, Lord, for being my stronghold. In the mighty and matchless name of Jesus, I pray, Amen.

Prayer 140: God's Promise of Peace

Scripture:

"You will keep him in perfect peace, whose mind is stayed on You, because he trusts in You."

(Isaiah 26:3 NKJV)

Prayer:

Father, I thank You for the promise of perfect peace. I choose to fix my mind on You today, trusting in Your goodness and faithfulness. Help me to stay focused on You, especially when the world around me feels chaotic.

Lord, when anxiety threatens to disrupt my peace, remind me to turn to You. Let Your peace guard my heart and mind, keeping me calm in the midst of uncertainty.

Thank You, Lord, for the perfect peace that comes from trusting in You. In the mighty and matchless name of Jesus, I pray, Amen.

Prayer 141: God's Abundant Provision

Scripture:

"And my God shall supply all your need according to His riches in glory by Christ Jesus."

(*Philippians 4:19 NKJV*)

Prayer:

Lord, I thank You for being my provider. You know my needs better than I do, and I trust that You will supply everything I require according to Your riches in glory. Help me to rest in that promise, knowing that You are always looking out for me.

Father, when I feel concerned about the future or uncertain about my needs, remind me of Your faithfulness. Let me walk in faith, confident that You are providing for me in every season.

Thank You, Lord, for Your abundant provision in my life. In the mighty and matchless name of Jesus, I pray, Amen.

Prayer 142: God's Hope in My Life

Scripture:

"For I know the thoughts that I think toward you, says the Lord, thoughts of peace and not of evil, to give you a future and a hope."

(Jeremiah 29:11 NKJV)

Prayer:

Father, I thank You for the hope You have promised me. Your thoughts towards me are good, and I trust that You are working everything for my future. Help me to hold onto that hope, especially when I feel discouraged or overwhelmed.

Lord, when I face uncertainty, remind me that You are in control and have a plan for my life. Let me look forward with confidence, knowing that You are leading me toward a bright future.

Thank You, Lord, for the hope You give me every day. In the mighty and matchless name of Jesus, I pray, Amen.

Prayer 143: God's Light in My Darkness

Scripture:

"The Lord is my light and my salvation; whom shall I fear? The Lord is the strength of my life; of whom shall I be afraid?"

(Psalm 27:1 NKJV)

Prayer:

Lord, I thank You for being my light and salvation. Your presence dispels fear and darkness in my life. Help me to walk in Your light, trusting that You will guide me through every challenge I face.

Father, when I feel afraid or uncertain, remind me that You are my strength. Let me find comfort in knowing that I am safe in Your care and that Your light leads the way.

Thank You, Lord, for being my light and my salvation. In the mighty and matchless name of Jesus, I pray, Amen.

Prayer 144: God's Rest for My Soul

Scripture:

"Come to Me, all you who labor and are heavy laden, and I will give you rest."

(Matthew 11:28 NKJV)

Prayer:

Father, I thank You for the invitation to come to You for rest. When I feel burdened by the cares of life, I can find refuge in Your presence. Help me to lay my worries at Your feet, trusting that You will provide the rest I need.

Lord, when I feel overwhelmed, remind me to turn to You. Let Your peace wash over me and bring rejuvenation to my spirit, allowing me to find comfort in Your embrace.

Thank You, Lord, for the rest You offer to my weary soul. In the mighty and matchless name of Jesus, I pray, Amen.

Prayer 145: God's Deliverance from Fear

Scripture:

"For God has not given us a spirit of fear, but of power and of love and of a sound mind."

(2 Timothy 1:7 NKJV)

Prayer:

Lord, I thank You for the power, love, and sound mind You have given me. I choose to reject any spirit of fear that tries to creep into my heart. Help me to stand firm in Your strength and to trust in Your promises.

Father, when fear threatens to overwhelm me, remind me of Your perfect love. Let me walk in confidence, knowing that You are my protector and that I can trust You completely.

Thank You, Lord, for delivering me from fear and filling me with Your peace. In the mighty and matchless name of Jesus, I pray, Amen.

Prayer 146: God's Joy in My Life

Scripture:

"The joy of the Lord is your strength."
(Nehemiah 8:10 NKJV)

Prayer:

Father, I thank You for the joy that comes from knowing You. Your joy is my strength, and I choose to embrace it today. Help me to find joy in every circumstance, knowing that You are always with me.

Lord, when I feel weighed down by the challenges of life, remind me to focus on the joy You provide. Let Your joy be my source of strength, lifting me up and enabling me to face each day with hope.

Thank You, Lord, for the joy that fills my heart. In the mighty and matchless name of Jesus, I pray, Amen.

Prayer 147: God's Purpose in My Life

Scripture:

"For we are His workmanship, created in Christ Jesus for good works, which God prepared beforehand that we should walk in them."

(Ephesians 2:10 NKJV)

Prayer:

Lord, I thank You for the unique purpose You have for my life. I am Your workmanship, and I trust that You have created me for good works. Help me to seek Your will and to walk in the plans You have laid out for me.

Father, when I feel unsure of my direction or purpose, remind me that I am fearfully and wonderfully made. Let me embrace the good works You have prepared for me, walking in faith and confidence.

Thank You, Lord, for the purpose You have instilled in me. In the mighty and matchless name of Jesus, I pray, Amen.

Prayer 148: God's Assurance of His Love

Scripture:

"For I am convinced that neither death nor life, neither angels nor demons, neither the present nor the future, nor any powers, neither height nor depth, nor anything else in all creation, will be able to separate us from the love of God that is in Christ Jesus our Lord."

(Romans 8:38-39 NKJV)

Prayer:

Father, I thank You for the assurance of Your unconditional love. There is nothing that can separate me from Your love, and I am grateful for that truth. Help me to rest in Your love, knowing that it is constant and unwavering.

Lord, when I feel unworthy or disconnected, remind me of the depth of Your love. Let me embrace that love and allow it to flow through me, sharing it with others in my life.

Thank You, Lord, for Your everlasting love. In the mighty and matchless name of Jesus, I pray, Amen.

Prayer 149: God's Wisdom in My Decisions

Scripture:

"If any of you lacks wisdom, let him ask of God, who gives to all liberally and without reproach, and it will be given to him."

(James 1:5 NKJV)

Prayer:

Lord, I thank You for the promise of wisdom. I ask for Your guidance as I make decisions in my life. Help me to seek You first and to trust that You will provide the wisdom I need to navigate through challenges.

Father, when I feel uncertain or confused, remind me to turn to You for clarity. Let Your wisdom illuminate my path and guide my thoughts and actions.

Thank You, Lord, for being my source of wisdom. In the mighty and matchless name of Jesus, I pray, Amen.

Prayer 150: God's Grace in My Weakness

Scripture:

"But He said to me, 'My grace is sufficient for you, for My strength is made perfect in weakness.' Therefore most gladly I will rather boast in my infirmities, that the power of Christ may rest upon me."

(2 Corinthians 12:9 NKJV)

Prayer:

Father, I thank You for Your grace that is sufficient for every need. In my weaknesses, I find strength in You. Help me to embrace my limitations and rely on Your power to accomplish what I cannot do on my own.

Lord, when I feel inadequate, remind me that Your strength is made perfect in my weakness. Let me walk in confidence, knowing that I am empowered by Your grace.

Thank You, Lord, for Your sufficient grace in my life. In the mighty and matchless name of Jesus, I pray, Amen.

Prayer 151: God's Promises of Restoration

Scripture:

"And I will restore to you the years that the swarming locust has eaten."

(Joel 2:25 NKJV)

Prayer:

Lord, I thank You for Your promise of restoration. No matter what I have lost, I trust that You can bring healing and renewal to my life. Help me to have faith in Your ability to restore what has been broken.

Father, when I look back on my past and see pain or loss, remind me that You can redeem those experiences. Let me walk forward with hope, knowing that You are working to restore and renew.

Thank You, Lord, for the gift of restoration. In the mighty and matchless name of Jesus, I pray, Amen.

Prayer 152: God's Faithfulness in Every Circumstance

Scripture:

"The steadfast love of the Lord never ceases; His mercies never come to an end; they are new every morning; great is Your faithfulness."

> *(Lamentations 3:22-23 NKJV)*

Prayer:

Father, I thank You for Your steadfast love and mercy that is new every morning. I can always count on Your faithfulness, no matter the circumstances I face. Help me to wake up each day with a heart full of gratitude for Your endless grace.

Lord, when I feel discouraged or overwhelmed, remind me of Your faithfulness. Let me cling to the truth that You are always working for my good.

Thank You, Lord, for Your unwavering faithfulness. In the mighty and matchless name of Jesus, I pray, Amen.

Prayer 153: God's Goodness in My Life

Scripture:

"Oh, taste and see that the Lord is good; blessed is the man who trusts in Him."

(Psalm 34:8 NKJV)

Prayer:

Father, I thank You for Your goodness in my life. I have tasted and seen that You are good, and I am grateful for all the blessings You have provided. Help me to continually trust in You, experiencing the richness of Your goodness every day.

Lord, when I feel discouraged, remind me of Your past faithfulness. Let me dwell on the many ways You have blessed me and draw me closer to You.

Thank You, Lord, for Your goodness and grace. In the mighty and matchless name of Jesus, I pray, Amen.

Prayer 154: God's Assurance in Times of Trouble

Scripture:

"Fear not, for I have redeemed you; I have called you by your name; you are Mine."

(Isaiah 43:1 NKJV)

Prayer:

Father, I thank You for the assurance that I am Yours. You have redeemed me and called me by name, and I can trust that I am safe in Your care. Help me to remember this truth when fear and doubt try to take hold of my heart.

Lord, when I face troubles, remind me that I belong to You. Let me walk confidently, knowing that You are with me in every situation and that I have nothing to fear.

Thank You, Lord, for calling me by name and for being my Redeemer. In the mighty and matchless name of Jesus, I pray, Amen.

Prayer 155: God's Encouragement in the Journey

Scripture:

"So be strong and courageous! Do not be afraid and do not panic before them. For the Lord your God will personally go ahead of you. He will neither fail you nor abandon you."
(Deuteronomy 31:6 NLT)

Prayer:

Lord, I thank You for Your encouragement to be strong and courageous. I know that You are with me every step of the way, going ahead to prepare my path. Help me to trust in Your presence and to remain fearless, even in the face of challenges.

Father, when I feel overwhelmed or tempted to give up, remind me of Your faithfulness. Let me find strength in knowing that You will never fail or abandon me.

Thank You, Lord, for walking with me on this journey. In the mighty and matchless name of Jesus, I pray, Amen.

Prayer 156: God's Joy in My Heart

Scripture:

"You make known to me the path of life; in Your presence there is fullness of joy; at Your right hand are pleasures forevermore."

(Psalm 16:11 ESV)

Prayer:

Father, I thank You for revealing the path of life to me. In Your presence, I find true joy that fills my heart to overflowing. Help me to seek Your presence daily, knowing that joy is found in communion with You.

Lord, when I feel discouraged or lost, remind me of the joy that comes from being with You. Let me experience the fullness of Your joy, allowing it to sustain me through every season of life.

Thank You, Lord, for the joy that comes from Your presence. In the mighty and matchless name of Jesus, I pray, Amen.

Prayer 157: God's Promises in My Life

Scripture:

"The Lord is not slack concerning His promise, as some count slackness, but is longsuffering toward us, not willing that any should perish but that all should come to repentance."

(2 Peter 3:9 NKJV)

Prayer:

Father, I thank You for Your promises that are always fulfilled. You are faithful and patient, desiring that none of us should perish. Help me to trust in Your timing and to wait expectantly for the fulfillment of Your promises in my life.

Lord, when I feel impatient or doubtful, remind me of Your faithfulness. Let me hold onto the truth that You are working for my good, and I can trust in Your plans.

Thank You, Lord, for Your enduring promises. In the mighty and matchless name of Jesus, I pray, Amen.

Prayer 158: God's Hope in Every Situation

Scripture:

"And hope does not disappoint us, because God has poured out His love into our hearts by the Holy Spirit, whom He has given us."

(Romans 5:5 NIV)

Prayer:

Lord, I thank You for the hope that does not disappoint. You have poured Your love into my heart through the Holy Spirit, and I can trust that my hope in You is secure. Help me to cling to that hope, especially during difficult times.

Father, when I feel overwhelmed or discouraged, remind me of Your love and faithfulness. Let my heart be filled with hope, knowing that You are always at work in my life.

Thank You, Lord, for the hope that sustains me. In the mighty and matchless name of Jesus, I pray, Amen.

Prayer 159: God's Love is Unchanging

Scripture:

"For I am convinced that neither death nor life, neither angels nor demons, neither the present nor the future, nor any powers, neither height nor depth, nor anything else in all creation, will be able to separate us from the love of God that is in Christ Jesus our Lord."

(Romans 8:38-39 NIV)

Prayer:

Father, I thank You for the assurance that nothing can separate me from Your love. Your love is unchanging and everlasting, and I am grateful for that truth. Help me to fully embrace Your love and to share it with others.

Lord, when I feel distant or unworthy, remind me of the depth of Your love for me. Let me rest in the assurance that I am forever loved and accepted by You.

Thank You, Lord, for Your unchanging love. In the mighty and matchless name of Jesus, I pray, Amen.

Prayer 160: God's Strength in My Weakness

Scripture:

"He gives power to the weak, and to those who have no might He increases strength."

(Isaiah 40:29 NKJV)

Prayer:

Lord, I thank You for the strength You provide in my weakness. When I feel exhausted or overwhelmed, I trust that You will empower me to keep going. Help me to lean on Your strength, knowing that it is sufficient for every challenge I face.

Father, when I am weary, remind me to turn to You for rejuvenation. Let me find strength in Your presence, allowing me to rise above my difficulties and walk in faith.

Thank You, Lord, for being my source of strength. In the mighty and matchless name of Jesus, I pray, Amen.

Prayer 161: God's Comfort in Sorrow

Scripture:

"Blessed are those who mourn, for they shall be comforted."
(Matthew 5:4 NKJV)

Prayer:

Father, I thank You for the comfort You promise to those who mourn. In times of sorrow, I can turn to You for solace and healing. Help me to seek Your presence in my grief, trusting that You will bring peace to my heart.

Lord, when I feel overwhelmed by loss or sadness, remind me of Your comforting presence. Let me find refuge in You, allowing Your love to surround me and bring me hope.

Thank You, Lord, for being my comforter in times of sorrow. In the mighty and matchless name of Jesus, I pray, Amen.

Prayer 162: God's Faithfulness in Every Season

Scripture:

"Jesus Christ is the same yesterday, today, and forever."
(Hebrews 13:8 NKJV)

Prayer:

Lord, I thank You for Your unwavering faithfulness. You are the same yesterday, today, and forever, and I can always trust in Your promises. Help me to remember this truth when life feels unpredictable or challenging.

Father, when I face trials, remind me that You are always with me. Let me lean on Your strength and find comfort in knowing that Your character never changes.

Thank You, Lord, for Your steadfast faithfulness. In the mighty and matchless name of Jesus, I pray, Amen.

Prayer 163: God's Abundant Mercy

Scripture:

"But God, who is rich in mercy, because of His great love with which He loved us."

(Ephesians 2:4 NKJV)

Prayer:

Father, I thank You for Your rich mercy and great love. Your compassion toward me is boundless, and I am forever grateful for Your grace. Help me to live in the light of that mercy, extending it to others as You have done for me.

Lord, when I feel undeserving or overwhelmed by guilt, remind me of Your mercy that covers my sins. Let me walk in the freedom that comes from knowing I am forgiven.

Thank You, Lord, for Your abundant mercy. In the mighty and matchless name of Jesus, I pray, Amen.

Prayer 164: God's Strength in Trials

Scripture:

"When you pass through the waters, I will be with you; and through the rivers, they shall not overflow you. When you walk through the fire, you shall not be burned, nor shall the flame scorch you."
(Isaiah 43:2 NKJV)

Prayer:

Lord, I thank You for Your promise to be with me in times of trouble. No matter the challenges I face, I know that You are always by my side, providing strength and protection. Help me to lean on You when the waters rise and the fires burn.

Father, when I feel overwhelmed by my circumstances, remind me of Your presence. Let me walk confidently, knowing that You are with me, guiding me through every trial.

Thank You, Lord, for Your unwavering support in my life. In the mighty and matchless name of Jesus, I pray, Amen.

Prayer 165: God's Promise of Restoration

Scripture:

"And I will restore to you the years that the swarming locust has eaten."

(Joel 2:25 NKJV)

Prayer:

Father, I thank You for Your promise of restoration. You can redeem the time that has been lost and bring healing to my heart. Help me to believe in Your ability to restore what has been broken in my life.

Lord, when I reflect on past losses or pain, remind me that You are a God of renewal. Let me look forward with hope, trusting that You are at work to bring about restoration.

Thank You, Lord, for the promise of healing and renewal. In the mighty and matchless name of Jesus, I pray, Amen.

Prayer 166: God's Faithfulness in Every Challenge

Scripture:

"The Lord is my strength and my shield; my heart trusts in Him, and I am helped therefore my heart exults, and with my song I shall thank Him."

(Psalm 28:7 KJV)

Prayer:

Father, I thank You for being my strength and shield in every challenge I face. My heart trusts in You, knowing that You are my helper and protector. Help me to remember this truth when I feel weak or afraid.

Lord, when I encounter difficulties, remind me that my trust in You is my greatest strength. Let my heart be filled with gratitude, and may I always sing praises to You for Your faithfulness.

Thank You, Lord, for being my strength and shield. In the mighty and matchless name of Jesus, I pray, Amen.

Prayer 167: God's Light in the Darkness

Scripture:

"The light shines in the darkness, and the darkness has not overcome it."

(John 1:5 ESV)

Prayer:

Lord, I thank You for being the light that shines in my darkness. No matter what challenges I face, Your light cannot be extinguished. Help me to seek Your light in every situation, trusting that it will guide me through.

Father, when I feel surrounded by darkness, remind me that Your light is always with me. Let me walk confidently in Your truth, shining Your light to others in need.

Thank You, Lord, for the light that overcomes all darkness. In the mighty and matchless name of Jesus, I pray, Amen.

Prayer 168: God's Abiding Presence

Scripture:

"And behold, I am with you always, to the end of the age."
(Matthew 28:20 ESV)

Prayer:

Father, I thank You for the promise of Your abiding presence. You are with me always, no matter where I go or what I face. Help me to feel Your presence in my life and to trust in Your constant companionship.

Lord, when I feel lonely or afraid, remind me that You are always by my side. Let me find comfort in knowing that I am never alone, and that You are walking with me through every trial.

Thank You, Lord, for Your faithful presence. In the mighty and matchless name of Jesus, I pray, Amen.

Prayer 169: God's Goodness in My Life

Scripture:

"Give thanks to the Lord, for He is good; His love endures forever."

(Psalm 136:1 NLT)

Prayer:

Father, I thank You for Your goodness and enduring love. Your faithfulness to me is unwavering, and I am so grateful for all the blessings You have given. Help me to live with a heart of gratitude, recognizing Your goodness in every aspect of my life.

Lord, when I feel discouraged, remind me of Your countless acts of kindness. Let me remember to give thanks for Your love and grace, and may that gratitude overflow into my interactions with others.

Thank You, Lord, for Your goodness that never fades. In the mighty and matchless name of Jesus, I pray, Amen.

Prayer 170: God's Promise of Healing

Scripture:

"He sent His word and healed them, and delivered them from their destructions."

(Psalm 107:20 KJV)

Prayer:

Father, I thank You for the healing that comes through Your Word. You sent Your Word to heal and deliver, and I trust in Your power to restore my body, mind, and spirit. Help me to seek Your healing touch in my life.

Lord, when I feel weak or unwell, remind me of the promises of restoration and health found in Your Word. Let my faith be strengthened as I trust in Your ability to heal.

Thank You, Lord, for the healing power of Your Word. In the mighty and matchless name of Jesus, I pray, Amen.

Prayer 171: God's Grace in My Weakness

Scripture:

"My grace is sufficient for you, for my power is made perfect in weakness."

(2 Corinthians 12:9 ESV)

Prayer:

Lord, I thank You for Your grace that is sufficient in my weakness. In times when I feel inadequate, I can lean on Your strength. Help me to embrace my limitations and rely on Your power to guide me through.

Father, when I feel overwhelmed, remind me that Your grace is enough. Let me find comfort in knowing that Your power is magnified in my weakness.

Thank You, Lord, for Your grace that sustains me. In the mighty and matchless name of Jesus, I pray, Amen.

Prayer 172: God's Promise of Peace

Scripture:

"Peace I leave with you, My peace I give to you; not as the world gives do I give to you. Let not your heart be troubled, neither let it be afraid."

(John 14:27 NKJV)

Prayer:

Father, I thank You for the peace that only You can give. Your peace is different from what the world offers, and I choose to receive it today. Help me to let go of any fears or worries that try to take root in my heart.

Lord, when anxiety threatens to disrupt my peace, remind me to turn to You. Let Your peace guard my heart and mind, allowing me to rest in Your presence.

Thank You, Lord, for the peace that surpasses all understanding. In the mighty and matchless name of Jesus, I pray, Amen.

Prayer 173: God's Power in My Life

Scripture:

"But you shall receive power when the Holy Spirit has come upon you; and you shall be witnesses to Me in Jerusalem, and in all Judea and Samaria, and to the end of the earth."
(Acts 1:8 NKJV)

Prayer:

Father, I thank You for the power of the Holy Spirit in my life. You have equipped me to be a witness for You, and I trust that Your Spirit empowers me to accomplish Your will. Help me to walk in that power every day.

Lord, when I feel inadequate or weak, remind me that Your Spirit is within me. Let me rely on that power to share Your love and truth with those around me.

Thank You, Lord, for the gift of the Holy Spirit and the power that comes from You. In the mighty and matchless name of Jesus, I pray, Amen.

Prayer 174: God's Faithfulness in Difficult Times

Scripture:

"The Lord is good to those who wait for Him, to the soul who seeks Him."

(Lamentations 3:25 ESV)

Prayer:

Lord, I thank You for Your goodness, especially in times of waiting. I trust that You are working behind the scenes for my good. Help me to be patient and to seek You during these times, knowing that You are faithful.

Father, when I feel anxious about the future or restless in my waiting, remind me that Your timing is perfect. Let me find peace in the process, trusting that You have a plan for my life.

Thank You, Lord, for Your faithfulness in every season. In the mighty and matchless name of Jesus, I pray, Amen.

Prayer 175: God's Protection Over My Life

Scripture:

"The Lord will protect you from all evil; He will keep your soul."

(Psalm 121:7 ESV)

Prayer:

Father, I thank You for Your promise of protection over my life. You are my shield and my fortress, guarding me from harm. Help me to rest in that assurance, knowing that You are always watching over me.

Lord, when I feel anxious about my safety or well-being, remind me of Your protective hand. Let me walk in confidence, trusting that You are my guardian in every situation.

Thank You, Lord, for Your protection that surrounds me. In the mighty and matchless name of Jesus, I pray, Amen.

Prayer 176: God's Provision in Every Need

Scripture:

"And God shall supply all your need according to His riches in glory by Christ Jesus."
(Philippians 4:19 KJV)

Prayer:

Father, I thank You for the promise of provision. You know my needs better than I do, and I trust that You will supply everything I require. Help me to rest in that promise and to seek You first in all things.

Lord, when I feel anxious about my needs or my future, remind me of Your faithfulness to provide. Let me walk in faith, confident that You are meeting every need according to Your riches in glory.

Thank You, Lord, for Your abundant provision in my life. In the mighty and matchless name of Jesus, I pray, Amen.

Prayer 177: God's Comfort in My Pain

Scripture:

"He heals the brokenhearted and binds up their wounds."
(Psalm 147:3 ESV)

Prayer:

Father, I thank You for being my healer. You see my pain and brokenness, and I trust that You are able to mend my heart and restore my soul. Help me to bring my wounds to You, knowing that You care deeply for me.

Lord, when I feel overwhelmed by grief or hurt, remind me of Your promise to heal. Let Your loving presence bring comfort and restoration to every area of my life.

Thank You, Lord, for Your healing power and compassion. In the mighty and matchless name of Jesus, I pray, Amen.

Prayer 178: God's Wisdom in Every Decision

Scripture:

"If any of you lacks wisdom, let him ask of God, who gives to all liberally and without reproach, and it will be given to him."

(James 1:5 KJV)

Prayer:

Lord, I thank You for the gift of wisdom that comes from You. I ask for Your guidance in every decision I face, trusting that You will provide the understanding I need. Help me to seek You first and to trust in Your ways.

Father, when I feel confused or uncertain, remind me to turn to You for clarity. Let Your wisdom guide my thoughts and actions, leading me toward what is best.

Thank You, Lord, for being my source of wisdom. In the mighty and matchless name of Jesus, I pray, Amen.

Prayer 179: God's Strength in My Weakness

Scripture:

"My grace is sufficient for you, for my power is made perfect in weakness."

(2 Corinthians 12:9 ESV)

Prayer:

Father, I thank You for Your grace that is sufficient for every need. In my weaknesses, I find strength in You. Help me to embrace my limitations and rely on Your power to guide me through.

Lord, when I feel overwhelmed or inadequate, remind me that Your strength is made perfect in my weakness. Let me walk in confidence, knowing that I am empowered by Your grace.

Thank You, Lord, for Your sufficient grace in my life. In the mighty and matchless name of Jesus, I pray, Amen.

Prayer 180: God's Goodness in All Things

Scripture:

"And we know that all things work together for good to those who love God, to those who are the called according to His purpose."

(Romans 8:28 KJV)

Prayer:

Father, I thank You for Your goodness and for the assurance that all things work together for good. I trust that even in difficult times, You are at work for my benefit. Help me to see Your hand in every situation and to remain steadfast in my love for You.

Lord, when I encounter challenges, remind me to keep my eyes on You. Let me find peace in knowing that You have a purpose for every circumstance I face.

Thank You, Lord, for Your goodness that prevails in my life. In the mighty and matchless name of Jesus, I pray, Amen.

Prayer 181: God's Peace in Troubling Times

Scripture:

"Peace I leave with you, My peace I give to you; not as the world gives do I give to you. Let not your heart be troubled, neither let it be afraid."

(John 14:27 KJV)

Prayer:

Lord, I thank You for the gift of peace. Your peace is different from what the world offers, and I choose to receive it today. Help me to let go of any fears or worries that try to take root in my heart.

Father, when anxiety threatens to disrupt my peace, remind me to turn to You. Let Your peace fill my heart and mind, allowing me to rest in Your presence.

Thank You, Lord, for the peace that surpasses all understanding. In the mighty and matchless name of Jesus, I pray, Amen.

Prayer 182: God's Faithfulness Through Every Season

Scripture:

"The steadfast love of the Lord never ceases; His mercies never come to an end; they are new every morning; great is Your faithfulness."

(Lamentations 3:22-23 ESV)

Prayer:

Father, I thank You for Your steadfast love and mercy. Each day is a new opportunity to experience Your grace, and I am so grateful for that. Help me to wake up with a heart full of gratitude, ready to embrace the new day You have given.

Lord, when I feel discouraged or overwhelmed, remind me of Your faithfulness. Let me cling to the truth that You are always working for my good.

Thank You, Lord, for Your unwavering faithfulness. In the mighty and matchless name of Jesus, I pray, Amen.

Prayer 183: God's Restoration in My Life

Scripture:

"And I will restore to you the years that the swarming locust has eaten."

(Joel 2:25 KJV)

Prayer:

Father, I thank You for Your promise of restoration. No matter what I have lost or what has been taken from me, I trust that You can restore it. Help me to believe in Your power to heal and to bring back the joy I once had.

Lord, when I reflect on my past losses, remind me that You are a God of renewal. Let me walk forward with hope, knowing that You are working to restore and renew my life.

Thank You, Lord, for the promise of restoration. In the mighty and matchless name of Jesus, I pray, Amen.

Prayer 184: God's Love is Unchanging

Scripture:

"But God demonstrates His own love toward us, in that while we were still sinners, Christ died for us."
(Romans 5:8 ESV)

Prayer:

Father, I thank You for the incredible love You have shown me through Christ. Your love is unchanging, and I am forever grateful for that assurance. Help me to fully grasp the depth of that love and to share it with others.

Lord, when I feel unworthy or disconnected, remind me of the depth of Your love. Let me rest in the truth that I am loved and accepted just as I am.

Thank You, Lord, for Your unchanging love. In the mighty and matchless name of Jesus, I pray, Amen.

Prayer 185: God's Wisdom in My Decisions

Scripture:

"The fear of the Lord is the beginning of wisdom, and the knowledge of the Holy One is understanding."
(Proverbs 9:10 NKJV)

Prayer:

Lord, I thank You for the wisdom that comes from fearing You. Help me to seek You in every decision I make, knowing that true understanding begins with a relationship with You.

Father, when I feel uncertain or confused, remind me to turn to Your Word for guidance. Let Your wisdom illuminate my path and help me to make choices that honor You.

Thank You, Lord, for the gift of wisdom in my life. In the mighty and matchless name of Jesus, I pray, Amen.

Prayer 186: God's Protection Over My Life

Scripture:

"The Lord is my fortress, my God, in whom I trust."
(Psalm 91:2 NIV)

Prayer:

Father, I thank You for being my fortress and protector. I trust in Your ability to keep me safe from harm. Help me to rely on Your strength and to find refuge in Your presence.

Lord, when I feel vulnerable or afraid, remind me that You are my stronghold. Let me walk confidently, knowing that You are shielding me from danger and guiding my steps.

Thank You, Lord, for Your protection that surrounds me. In the mighty and matchless name of Jesus, I pray, Amen.

Prayer 187: God's Faithfulness in My Life

Scripture:

"For the Lord your God is God, the faithful God who keeps covenant and steadfast love with those who love Him and keep His commandments, to a thousand generations."
(Deuteronomy 7:9 ESV)

Prayer:

Lord, I thank You for Your faithfulness that endures through generations. You are a God of covenant, and I trust in Your steadfast love. Help me to remain faithful to You, knowing that Your promises are true.

Father, when I feel doubt or fear creeping in, remind me of Your past faithfulness. Let me cling to the truth that You are always with me, fulfilling Your promises in my life.

Thank You, Lord, for Your faithfulness that never fails. In the mighty and matchless name of Jesus, I pray, Amen.

Prayer 188: God's Goodness in Every Situation

Scripture:

"Oh, give thanks to the Lord, for He is good! For His mercy endures forever."

(Psalm 107:1 NKJV)

Prayer:

Father, I thank You for Your goodness that is evident in my life. Your mercy endures forever, and I am grateful for all the blessings You provide. Help me to cultivate a heart of gratitude, recognizing Your goodness in every situation.

Lord, when I feel discouraged, remind me of the many ways You have been faithful. Let me praise You for Your goodness, and may my heart overflow with thankfulness.

Thank You, Lord, for Your goodness that never fades. In the mighty and matchless name of Jesus, I pray, Amen.

Prayer 189: God's Hope in My Heart

Scripture:

"For I know the thoughts that I think toward you, says the Lord, thoughts of peace and not of evil, to give you a future and a hope."

(Jeremiah 29:11 KJV)

Prayer:

Father, I thank You for the hope You have promised. Your thoughts toward me are good, and I trust that You are working everything for my future. Help me to hold onto that hope, especially when I feel discouraged.

Lord, when I feel lost or unsure, remind me that You are in control and have a plan for my life. Let me look forward with confidence, knowing that You are leading me toward a bright future.

Thank You, Lord, for the hope that sustains me each day. In the mighty and matchless name of Jesus, I pray, Amen.

Prayer 190: God's Strength in My Journey

Scripture:

"I can do all things through Christ who strengthens me."
(Philippians 4:13 KJV)

Prayer:

Lord, I thank You for the strength that comes from Christ. I can face any challenge because You empower me. Help me to rely on Your strength and to trust in Your ability to carry me through every situation.

Father, when I feel weak or overwhelmed, remind me that I can do all things through You. Let me walk confidently, knowing that Your power is at work within me.

Thank You, Lord, for the strength that sustains me in my journey. In the mighty and matchless name of Jesus, I pray, Amen.

Prayer 191: God's Assurance in Trials

Scripture:

"The Lord is close to the brokenhearted and saves those who are crushed in spirit."
(Psalm 34:18 NIV)

Prayer:

Father, I thank You for being close to me in my times of trial. You see my heartaches and struggles, and I trust that You will bring healing and restoration. Help me to lean on You when I feel broken, knowing that You are with me every step of the way.

Lord, when I feel overwhelmed by my circumstances, remind me of Your promise to be near. Let me find comfort in Your presence, allowing You to mend my broken heart.

Thank You, Lord, for Your unwavering support in my trials. In the mighty and matchless name of Jesus, I pray, Amen.

Prayer 192: God's Goodness in All Things

Scripture:

"Give thanks to the Lord, for He is good; His love endures forever."

(Psalm 136:1 NLT)

Prayer:

Lord, I thank You for Your goodness and love that endure forever. Your faithfulness is evident in my life, and I am grateful for all the blessings You provide. Help me to cultivate a heart of gratitude and to recognize Your goodness in every situation.

Father, when I feel discouraged, remind me of the countless ways You have shown Your love. Let me dwell on Your goodness and share it with others around me.

Thank You, Lord, for Your unchanging goodness. In the mighty and matchless name of Jesus, I pray, Amen.

Prayer 193: God's Comfort in Grief

Scripture:

"He will wipe every tear from their eyes, and there will be no more death or sorrow or crying or pain. All these things are gone forever."

(Revelation 21:4 NLT)

Prayer:

Father, I thank You for the promise of ultimate comfort and healing. In times of grief, I hold onto the hope that one day, all pain and sorrow will be erased. Help me to find solace in Your presence as I navigate through my current heartaches.

Lord, when I feel overwhelmed by sadness, remind me of Your love and the promise of restoration. Let Your peace fill my heart, bringing comfort and strength during this difficult time.

Thank You, Lord, for being my comforter in grief. In the mighty and matchless name of Jesus, I pray, Amen.

Prayer 194: God's Guidance in My Life

Scripture:

"Trust in the Lord with all your heart, and do not lean on your own understanding. In all your ways acknowledge Him, and He will make straight your paths."

(Proverbs 3:5-6 ESV)

Prayer:

Lord, I thank You for Your guidance in my life. I choose to trust You with my whole heart, knowing that You are leading me on the right path. Help me to seek Your wisdom in every decision I make and to rely on Your understanding rather than my own.

Father, when I feel uncertain or confused, remind me to lean on You. Let me acknowledge You in all my ways, confident that You will direct my steps.

Thank You, Lord, for Your faithful guidance. In the mighty and matchless name of Jesus, I pray, Amen.

Prayer 195: God's Restoration in My Life

Scripture:

"For I will restore health to you, and your wounds I will heal, says the Lord."

(Jeremiah 30:17 ESV)

Prayer:

Father, I thank You for Your promise of restoration. You are the God who heals and restores, and I trust in Your power to mend my brokenness. Help me to bring my wounds before You, knowing that You care deeply for my heart.

Lord, when I feel discouraged or defeated, remind me that You are at work to heal me. Let me walk in faith, anticipating the restoration You have promised.

Thank You, Lord, for Your healing and restoration in my life. In the mighty and matchless name of Jesus, I pray, Amen.

Prayer 196: God's Faithfulness Through Every Season

Scripture:

"Jesus Christ is the same yesterday, today, and forever."
(Hebrews 13:8 ESV)

Prayer:

Lord, I thank You for Your unwavering faithfulness. You remain the same through every season of my life, and I can always count on You. Help me to remember this truth when life feels unpredictable or challenging.

Father, when I face trials, remind me that You are always with me. Let me lean on Your strength and find comfort in knowing that Your character never changes.

Thank You, Lord, for Your steadfast faithfulness. In the mighty and matchless name of Jesus, I pray, Amen.

Prayer 197: God's Joy in My Heart

Scripture:

"The joy of the Lord is your strength."
(Nehemiah 8:10 KJV)

Prayer:

Father, I thank You for the joy that comes from knowing You. Your joy is my strength, and I choose to embrace it today. Help me to find joy in every circumstance, trusting that You are always with me.

Lord, when I feel weighed down by the challenges of life, remind me of the joy You provide. Let Your joy be my source of strength, lifting me up and enabling me to face each day with hope.

Thank You, Lord, for the joy that fills my heart. In the mighty and matchless name of Jesus, I pray, Amen.

Prayer 198: God's Promises of Hope

Scripture:

"The Lord is good to those who wait for Him, to the soul who seeks Him."

(Lamentations 3:25 ESV)

Prayer:

Father, I thank You for Your goodness and the hope You provide. I choose to wait for You and seek You with all my heart. Help me to be patient and to trust in Your timing, knowing that You are always working for my good.

Lord, when I feel anxious about the future, remind me that You are in control. Let me find peace in the waiting, trusting that You have a plan for my life.

Thank You, Lord, for Your promises of hope and goodness. In the mighty and matchless name of Jesus, I pray, Amen.

Prayer 199: God's Abundant Grace

Scripture:

"But He said to me, 'My grace is sufficient for you, for my strength is made perfect in weakness.' Therefore most gladly I will rather boast in my infirmities, that the power of Christ may rest upon me."

(2 Corinthians 12:9 KJV)

Prayer:

Lord, I thank You for Your grace that is sufficient in every need. Your power shines through my weaknesses, reminding me that I am not alone. Help me to embrace my limitations and rely on Your strength to guide me through.

Father, when I feel overwhelmed or inadequate, remind me that Your grace covers me. Let me walk in confidence, knowing that I am empowered by Your love.

Thank You, Lord, for Your sufficient grace in my life. In the mighty and matchless name of Jesus, I pray, Amen.

Prayer 200: God's Love is Everlasting

Scripture:

"For I am convinced that neither death nor life, neither angels nor demons, neither the present nor the future, nor any powers, neither height nor depth, nor anything else in all creation, will be able to separate us from the love of God that is in Christ Jesus our Lord."

(Romans 8:38-39 ESV)

Prayer:

Father, I thank You for the assurance of Your everlasting love. Nothing can separate me from Your love, and I find comfort in that truth. Help me to fully embrace Your love and to share it with others around me.

Lord, when I feel unworthy or distant, remind me of the depth of Your love. Let me rest in the assurance that I am forever loved and accepted by You.

Thank You, Lord, for Your unchanging love. In the mighty and matchless name of Jesus, I pray, Amen.

Prayer 201: God's Presence in Times of Trouble

Scripture:

"God is our refuge and strength, a very present help in trouble."

(Psalm 46:1 KJV)

Prayer:

Father, I thank You for being my refuge and strength. In times of trouble, I can always turn to You for help. Help me to remember that You are my safe place, where I can find comfort and security.

Lord, when challenges arise, remind me of Your presence in my life. Let me lean on You, knowing that You are always there to guide and support me.

Thank You, Lord, for being my ever-present help in times of trouble. In the mighty and matchless name of Jesus, I pray, Amen.

Prayer 202: God's Hope for the Future

Scripture:

"For I know the plans I have for you, declares the Lord, plans to prosper you and not to harm you, plans to give you hope and a future."

(Jeremiah 29:11 NLT)

Prayer:

Lord, I thank You for the plans You have for my life. I trust that Your plans are good and filled with hope. Help me to hold onto that promise, especially during times of uncertainty.

Father, when I feel lost or anxious about the future, remind me that You are in control. Let me rest in the assurance that You are leading me toward a future filled with purpose.

Thank You, Lord, for Your hope and promise for my life. In the mighty and matchless name of Jesus, I pray, Amen.

Prayer 203: God's Strength in My Trials

Scripture:

"But He said to me, 'My grace is sufficient for you, for my power is made perfect in weakness.' Therefore I will boast all the more gladly about my weaknesses, so that Christ's power may rest on me."

(2 Corinthians 12:9 NIV)

Prayer:

Father, I thank You for the strength that comes from Your grace. In my weakness, I find Your power at work within me. Help me to embrace my struggles, knowing that they can be a source of strength through You.

Lord, when I feel inadequate or overwhelmed, remind me that Your grace is sufficient. Let me lean on You, trusting that Your power is made perfect in my weakness.

Thank You, Lord, for the strength that sustains me through my trials. In the mighty and matchless name of Jesus, I pray, Amen.

Prayer 204: God's Love for Me

Scripture:

"See what great love the Father has lavished on us, that we should be called children of God! And that is what we are!"
(1 John 3:1 NIV)

Prayer:

Father, I thank You for the incredible love You have shown me. Being called Your child is a precious gift, and I am grateful for Your unconditional love. Help me to fully embrace my identity as Your child and to walk in that love daily.

Lord, when I feel unworthy or distant, remind me of Your great love. Let me find comfort in knowing that I am cherished and accepted by You.

Thank You, Lord, for lavishing Your love upon me. In the mighty and matchless name of Jesus, I pray, Amen.

Prayer 205: God's Comfort in Sorrow

Scripture:

"Blessed are those who mourn, for they shall be comforted."
(Matthew 5:4 ESV)

Prayer:

Lord, I thank You for the promise of comfort for those who mourn. You see my pain and heartache, and I trust that You will bring healing to my wounds. Help me to seek Your comfort during these difficult times.

Father, when sorrow weighs heavily on my heart, remind me that You are near. Let me find solace in Your presence, allowing Your love to mend my brokenness.

Thank You, Lord, for being my comforter in times of grief. In the mighty and matchless name of Jesus, I pray, Amen.

Prayer 206: God's Guidance in My Life

Scripture:

"Trust in the Lord with all your heart and lean not on your own understanding; in all your ways submit to Him, and He will make your paths straight."

(Proverbs 3:5-6 NIV)

Prayer:

Father, I thank You for Your guidance in my life. I choose to trust in You with all my heart, knowing that You know what is best for me. Help me to submit my plans to You and to seek Your wisdom in every decision I make.

Lord, when I feel uncertain or confused, remind me to lean on Your understanding rather than my own. Let me walk in faith, trusting that You are directing my steps.

Thank You, Lord, for being my guide. In the mighty and matchless name of Jesus, I pray, Amen.

Prayer 207: God's Mercy and Grace

Scripture:

"The Lord is gracious and merciful; slow to anger and great in lovingkindness."

(Psalm 145:8 ESV)

Prayer:

Father, I thank You for Your mercy and grace that are new every morning. Your lovingkindness toward me is beyond measure, and I am so grateful for Your patience and compassion. Help me to extend that same grace to others in my life.

Lord, when I feel overwhelmed by guilt or shame, remind me of Your unfailing mercy. Let me walk in the freedom that comes from knowing I am forgiven and loved.

Thank You, Lord, for Your grace that sustains me. In the mighty and matchless name of Jesus, I pray, Amen.

Prayer 208: God's Protection Over My Heart

Scripture:

"Above all else, guard your heart, for everything you do flows from it."

(Proverbs 4:23 NIV)

Prayer:

Father, I thank You for the call to guard my heart. I know that my heart is precious to You, and I want to protect it from negativity and harm. Help me to be vigilant about what I allow into my heart and mind.

Lord, when I face temptation or doubt, remind me to turn to You for strength. Let me find refuge in Your love and truth, so that I can protect my heart from the things that seek to lead me astray.

Thank You, Lord, for being my protector. In the mighty and matchless name of Jesus, I pray, Amen.

Prayer 209: God's Joy in Every Season

Scripture:

"Rejoice in the Lord always. Again I will say, rejoice!"
(Philippians 4:4 ESV)

Prayer:

Father, I thank You for the joy that comes from knowing You. I choose to rejoice in You always, regardless of my circumstances. Help me to cultivate a spirit of joy that reflects Your goodness in my life.

Lord, when I feel overwhelmed by life's challenges, remind me to focus on the blessings You have given. Let my heart be filled with joy, allowing it to shine brightly for others to see.

Thank You, Lord, for the joy that sustains me. In the mighty and matchless name of Jesus, I pray, Amen.

Prayer 210: God's Assurance of His Love

Scripture:

"The Lord your God is in your midst, a mighty one who will save; He will rejoice over you with gladness; He will quiet you by His love; He will exult over you with loud singing."
(Zephaniah 3:17 ESV)

Prayer:

Father, I thank You for Your incredible love and joy. Knowing that You rejoice over me brings comfort to my heart. Help me to embrace that love and to live in the fullness of Your presence.

Lord, when I feel anxious or unworthy, remind me that You quiet my soul with Your love. Let me find peace in knowing that I am cherished and valued in Your eyes.

Thank You, Lord, for the assurance of Your love that comforts me. In the mighty and matchless name of Jesus, I pray, Amen.

Prayer 211: God's Strength in My Trials

Scripture:

"I can do all things through Christ who strengthens me."
(Philippians 4:13 KJV)

Prayer:

Father, I thank You for the strength You provide in every trial. I can face any challenge because You empower me. Help me to rely on Your strength and to trust in Your ability to carry me through.

Lord, when I feel weak or overwhelmed, remind me that I can do all things through You. Let me walk confidently, knowing that Your power is at work within me.

Thank You, Lord, for the strength that sustains me in my journey. In the mighty and matchless name of Jesus, I pray, Amen.

Prayer 212: God's Presence in Difficult Times

Scripture:

"When you pass through the waters, I will be with you; and through the rivers, they shall not overflow you."
(Isaiah 43:2 KJV)

Prayer:

Father, I thank You for the promise of Your presence during difficult times. No matter what challenges I face, I know that You are always with me. Help me to remember this truth when I feel overwhelmed.

Lord, when I feel like I'm drowning in my struggles, remind me that You are my refuge and strength. Let me find comfort in Your presence, knowing that You are guiding me through every trial.

Thank You, Lord, for being my constant companion. In the mighty and matchless name of Jesus, I pray, Amen.

Prayer 213: God's Assurance of His Love

Scripture:

"But God demonstrates His own love toward us, in that while we were still sinners, Christ died for us."
(Romans 5:8 NKJV)

Prayer:

Father, I thank You for the incredible love You have shown me through Christ. Your love is unconditional and sacrificial, and I am forever grateful for that assurance. Help me to fully grasp the depth of that love and to share it with others.

Lord, when I feel unworthy or distant, remind me of the depth of Your love. Let me rest in the assurance that I am loved and accepted by You, regardless of my shortcomings.

Thank You, Lord, for Your everlasting love. In the mighty and matchless name of Jesus, I pray, Amen.

Prayer 214: God's Healing Touch

Scripture:

"He heals the brokenhearted and binds up their wounds."
(Psalm 147:3 KJV)

Prayer:

Father, I thank You for Your healing touch in my life. You see my pain and brokenness, and I trust that You are able to mend my heart and restore my spirit. Help me to bring my wounds to You, knowing that You care for me.

Lord, when I feel overwhelmed by grief or hurt, remind me that You are with me to heal. Let Your loving presence bring comfort and restoration to every area of my life.

Thank You, Lord, for Your compassionate healing. In the mighty and matchless name of Jesus, I pray, Amen.

Prayer 215: God's Comfort in Sorrow

Scripture:

"Blessed are those who mourn, for they shall be comforted."
(Matthew 5:4 ESV)

Prayer:

Lord, I thank You for the promise of comfort for those who mourn. You understand my pain, and I trust that You will bring healing to my heart. Help me to seek Your comfort during these difficult times.

Father, when I feel overwhelmed by sorrow, remind me that You are near. Let me find refuge in Your love, allowing Your presence to mend my brokenness.

Thank You, Lord, for being my comforter in times of grief. In the mighty and matchless name of Jesus, I pray, Amen.

Prayer 216: God's Guidance in Every Step

Scripture:

"Your word is a lamp to my feet and a light to my path."
(Psalm 119:105 ESV)

Prayer:

Father, I thank You for the guidance found in Your Word. It illuminates my path and shows me the way I should go. Help me to seek Your Word daily, allowing it to direct my steps and decisions.

Lord, when I feel lost or uncertain, remind me to turn to Your truth. Let Your Word be my guide, providing clarity and direction in every aspect of my life.

Thank You, Lord, for the light of Your Word. In the mighty and matchless name of Jesus, I pray, Amen.

Prayer 217: God's Joy in My Life

Scripture:

"The joy of the Lord is your strength."
(Nehemiah 8:10 KJV)

Prayer:

Father, I thank You for the joy that comes from knowing You. Your joy is my strength, and I choose to embrace it today. Help me to find joy in every circumstance, trusting that You are always with me.

Lord, when I feel weighed down by life's challenges, remind me of the joy You provide. Let Your joy be my source of strength, uplifting my spirit and enabling me to face each day with hope.

Thank You, Lord, for the joy that fills my heart. In the mighty and matchless name of Jesus, I pray, Amen.

Prayer 218: God's Peace in Every Storm

Scripture:

"Peace I leave with you, My peace I give to you; not as the world gives do I give to you. Let not your heart be troubled, neither let it be afraid."

(John 14:27 NKJV)

Prayer:

Father, I thank You for the peace that You provide. It is not like the world's peace, but a deep, abiding peace that calms my heart. Help me to receive Your peace and to trust in Your goodness, even in the midst of chaos.

Lord, when anxiety threatens to disrupt my peace, remind me to turn to You. Let Your peace fill my heart and mind, allowing me to rest in Your presence.

Thank You, Lord, for the peace that surpasses all understanding. In the mighty and matchless name of Jesus, I pray, Amen.

Prayer 219: God's Faithfulness Through All Seasons

Scripture:

"The steadfast love of the Lord never ceases; His mercies never come to an end; they are new every morning; great is Your faithfulness."

(Lamentations 3:22-23 ESV)

Prayer:

Father, I thank You for Your steadfast love and mercies that are new every morning. I am grateful for Your faithfulness, which sustains me through every season of life. Help me to wake up with a heart full of gratitude, ready to embrace the new day You have given.

Lord, when I feel discouraged or overwhelmed, remind me of Your past faithfulness. Let me cling to the truth that You are always working for my good.

Thank You, Lord, for Your unwavering faithfulness. In the mighty and matchless name of Jesus, I pray, Amen.

Prayer 220: God's Purpose in My Life

Scripture:

"For we are His workmanship, created in Christ Jesus for good works, which God prepared beforehand that we should walk in them."

(Ephesians 2:10 ESV)

Prayer:

Father, I thank You for the unique purpose You have for my life. I am Your workmanship, created for good works. Help me to seek Your will and to walk in the plans You have laid out for me.

Lord, when I feel uncertain about my purpose, remind me that I am fearfully and wonderfully made. Let me embrace the good works You have prepared for me, walking in faith and confidence.

Thank You, Lord, for the purpose You have instilled in me. In the mighty and matchless name of Jesus, I pray, Amen.

Prayer 221: God's Healing Power

Scripture:

"And the prayer of faith will save the one who is sick, and the Lord will raise him up. And if he has committed sins, he will be forgiven."

(James 5:15 ESV)

Prayer:

Father, I thank You for the power of prayer and the healing it can bring. I trust that You are able to heal not only my body but also my spirit. Help me to bring my needs before You with faith, believing in Your ability to restore and revive.

Lord, when I or my loved ones face illness, remind me to seek You first. Let my prayers be filled with faith, knowing that You are the ultimate healer.

Thank You, Lord, for Your healing power in my life. In the mighty and matchless name of Jesus, I pray, Amen.

Prayer 222: God's Strength in Weakness

Scripture:

"He gives power to the weak, and to those who have no might He increases strength."

(Isaiah 40:29 NKJV)

Prayer:

Lord, I thank You for being the source of strength in my weakness. You provide power when I feel powerless, and I trust in Your ability to sustain me. Help me to lean on You when I feel overwhelmed or unable to continue.

Father, when I face challenges that seem insurmountable, remind me that Your strength is made perfect in my weakness. Let me find comfort in knowing that I am strong because of You.

Thank You, Lord, for the strength You give me daily. In the mighty and matchless name of Jesus, I pray, Amen.

Prayer 223: God's Love Endures Forever

Scripture:

"Give thanks to the Lord, for He is good; His love endures forever."

(Psalm 136:1 NIV)

Prayer:

Father, I thank You for Your enduring love. Your goodness is evident in my life, and I am grateful for Your constant presence. Help me to remember that Your love never fails and is always available to me.

Lord, when I feel unworthy or distant, remind me of Your everlasting love. Let me find comfort in knowing that no matter my circumstances, I am loved by You.

Thank You, Lord, for Your unchanging love that sustains me. In the mighty and matchless name of Jesus, I pray, Amen.

Prayer 224: God's Peace in the Midst of Chaos

Scripture:

"In peace I will both lie down and sleep; for you alone, O Lord, make me dwell in safety."

(Psalm 4:8 ESV)

Prayer:

Lord, I thank You for the peace that comes from knowing You are my protector. In times of chaos, I can find safety and rest in Your presence. Help me to lie down in peace, trusting in Your ability to keep me safe.

Father, when anxiety or fear tries to invade my mind, remind me to turn to You for comfort. Let Your peace guard my heart and mind, allowing me to sleep soundly in Your care.

Thank You, Lord, for the peace that sustains me in every situation. In the mighty and matchless name of Jesus, I pray, Amen.

Prayer 225: God's Promise of Restoration

Scripture:

"For I will restore health to you, and your wounds I will heal, says the Lord."

(Jeremiah 30:17 ESV)

Prayer:

Father, I thank You for Your promise of restoration. You are the God who heals and makes all things new. Help me to trust in Your ability to restore my heart and spirit, no matter what I have lost.

Lord, when I reflect on my past wounds, remind me that You are always at work to heal and renew. Let me walk forward in faith, anticipating the restoration You have promised.

Thank You, Lord, for Your healing touch and restoration in my life. In the mighty and matchless name of Jesus, I pray, Amen.

Prayer 226: God's Faithfulness in Every Trial

Scripture:

"Many are the afflictions of the righteous, but the Lord delivers him out of them all."

(Psalm 34:19 KJV)

Prayer:

Father, I thank You for Your faithfulness during trials. I know that even when I face difficulties, You are my deliverer. Help me to trust in Your promises and to find strength in You when I am in the midst of challenges.

Lord, when I feel overwhelmed, remind me of Your past deliverances. Let my faith be strengthened as I remember how You have always been there for me.

Thank You, Lord, for Your faithfulness through every trial I face. In the mighty and matchless name of Jesus, I pray, Amen.

Prayer 227: God's Abundant Grace

Scripture:

"For sin will have no dominion over you, since you are not under law but under grace."
(Romans 6:14 ESV)

Prayer:

Father, I thank You for Your abundant grace that covers my life. I am grateful that I am not bound by the law, but I live under Your grace. Help me to embrace that grace and to extend it to others as You have done for me.

Lord, when I struggle with sin or guilt, remind me that Your grace is sufficient. Let me walk in freedom, knowing that I am forgiven and empowered by Your love.

Thank You, Lord, for the grace that transforms my life. In the mighty and matchless name of Jesus, I pray, Amen.

Prayer 228: God's Guidance in Every Decision

Scripture:

"If any of you lacks wisdom, let him ask of God, who gives to all liberally and without reproach, and it will be given to him."

(James 1:5 NKJV)

Prayer:

Lord, I thank You for the promise of wisdom that comes from You. I ask for Your guidance in every decision I make, trusting that You will provide the understanding I need. Help me to seek You first in all things.

Father, when I feel uncertain or confused, remind me to turn to Your Word for guidance. Let Your wisdom illuminate my path, leading me in the right direction.

Thank You, Lord, for being my source of wisdom. In the mighty and matchless name of Jesus, I pray, Amen.

Prayer 229: God's Love is Everlasting

Scripture:

"The steadfast love of the Lord never ceases; His mercies never come to an end."

(Lamentations 3:22 ESV)

Prayer:

Father, I thank You for Your steadfast love that endures forever. Your mercies are new every morning, and I am so grateful for Your faithfulness. Help me to embrace that love and to share it with those around me.

Lord, when I feel distant or unworthy, remind me of the depth of Your love. Let me rest in the assurance that I am forever loved and accepted by You.

Thank You, Lord, for Your unchanging love. In the mighty and matchless name of Jesus, I pray, Amen.

Prayer 230: God's Assurance in Difficult Times

Scripture:

"The Lord is my shepherd; I shall not want. He makes me lie down in green pastures. He leads me beside still waters."
(Psalm 23:1-2 ESV)

Prayer:

Father, I thank You for being my Shepherd. You guide me and provide for my every need. Help me to trust in Your leading and to find rest in Your care.

Lord, when I feel anxious or uncertain, remind me that You are always watching over me. Let me find comfort in knowing that You are leading me to places of peace and restoration.

Thank You, Lord, for being my Shepherd. In the mighty and matchless name of Jesus, I pray, Amen.

Prayer 231: God's Hope in My Heart

Scripture:

"May the God of hope fill you with all joy and peace in believing, so that by the power of the Holy Spirit you may abound in hope."

(Romans 15:13 ESV)

Prayer:

Father, I thank You for being the God of hope. I ask that You fill my heart with joy and peace as I trust in You. Help me to rely on the power of the Holy Spirit, so that I may overflow with hope in every circumstance.

Lord, when I feel overwhelmed or discouraged, remind me that my hope is anchored in You. Let me be a beacon of hope to others, sharing the joy and peace I have found in Your presence.

Thank You, Lord, for the hope that sustains me. In the mighty and matchless name of Jesus, I pray, Amen.

Prayer 232: God's Abundant Provision

Scripture:

"And my God will supply every need of yours according to His riches in glory in Christ Jesus."

(Philippians 4:19 ESV)

Prayer:

Father, I thank You for Your promise to provide for all my needs. I trust in Your abundant resources and Your faithfulness to meet me where I am. Help me to remember that You are my provider in every situation.

Lord, when I feel anxious about the future or my needs, remind me of Your past provision. Let me walk in faith, confident that You are taking care of me.

Thank You, Lord, for supplying all my needs. In the mighty and matchless name of Jesus, I pray, Amen.

Prayer 233: God's Faithfulness in My Life

Scripture:

"Know therefore that the Lord your God is God; He is the faithful God, keeping His covenant of love to a thousand generations of those who love Him and keep His commandments."

(Deuteronomy 7:9 NIV)

Prayer:

Father, I thank You for Your faithfulness that spans generations. You are a God of love and promises, and I am grateful to be a recipient of Your grace. Help me to remain faithful to You, honoring the covenant You have made with me.

Lord, when I feel uncertain about my circumstances, remind me of Your unwavering faithfulness. Let me find comfort in knowing that You are always working for my good.

Thank You, Lord, for Your enduring faithfulness. In the mighty and matchless name of Jesus, I pray, Amen.

Prayer 234: God's Joy in My Journey

Scripture:

"Delight yourself in the Lord, and He will give you the desires of your heart."

(Psalm 37:4 ESV)

Prayer:

Father, I thank You for the joy that comes from delighting in You. As I seek You first, I trust that You will align my heart with Your will. Help me to find joy in my journey, knowing that You are guiding my steps.

Lord, when I feel distracted by life's challenges, remind me to focus on You. Let my heart be filled with joy as I pursue my relationship with You.

Thank You, Lord, for the joy that fills my heart. In the mighty and matchless name of Jesus, I pray, Amen.

Prayer 235: God's Comfort in My Life

Scripture:

"The Lord is near to the brokenhearted and saves the crushed in spirit."

(Psalm 34:18 ESV)

Prayer:

Father, I thank You for being near to me in my times of sorrow. You see my pain, and I trust that You will bring healing to my heart. Help me to seek Your comfort in my struggles, knowing that You are always present.

Lord, when I feel crushed by grief or disappointment, remind me that You are my refuge. Let me find solace in Your presence, allowing Your love to mend my brokenness.

Thank You, Lord, for the comfort You provide. In the mighty and matchless name of Jesus, I pray, Amen.

Prayer 236: God's Light in My Life

Scripture:

"Your word is a lamp to my feet and a light to my path."
(Psalm 119:105 ESV)

Prayer:

Father, I thank You for the guidance found in Your Word. It illuminates my path and shows me the way I should go. Help me to seek Your Word daily, allowing it to direct my steps and decisions.

Lord, when I feel lost or uncertain, remind me to turn to Your truth. Let Your Word be my guide, providing clarity and direction in every aspect of my life.

Thank You, Lord, for the light of Your Word. In the mighty and matchless name of Jesus, I pray, Amen.

Prayer 237: God's Assurance of His Presence

Scripture:

"And behold, I am with you always, to the end of the age."
(Matthew 28:20 ESV)

Prayer:

Father, I thank You for the assurance of Your presence in my life. You are always with me, guiding and protecting me. Help me to be aware of Your presence in every moment, especially during times of uncertainty.

Lord, when I feel alone or afraid, remind me that You are by my side. Let me find comfort in the knowledge that I am never without Your support.

Thank You, Lord, for being my constant companion. In the mighty and matchless name of Jesus, I pray, Amen.

Prayer 238: God's Purpose for My Life

Scripture:

"For I know the plans I have for you, declares the Lord, plans to prosper you and not to harm you, plans to give you hope and a future."

(Jeremiah 29:11 NIV)

Prayer:

Father, I thank You for the wonderful plans You have for my life. I trust that Your intentions are good and filled with hope. Help me to seek Your will and to follow the path You have laid out for me.

Lord, when I feel uncertain about my future, remind me that You are guiding me toward a purpose greater than I can see. Let me walk in faith, believing in Your promises.

Thank You, Lord, for the hope and future You have prepared for me. In the mighty and matchless name of Jesus, I pray, Amen.

Prayer 239: God's Love in My Relationships

Scripture:

"Above all, love each other deeply, because love covers over a multitude of sins."

(1 Peter 4:8 NIV)

Prayer:

Father, I thank You for the gift of love in my relationships. Help me to love others deeply and selflessly, just as You have loved me. Teach me to extend grace and forgiveness, allowing love to prevail in all my interactions.

Lord, when I encounter conflict or frustration in my relationships, remind me of the power of love. Let me choose to respond with kindness and understanding, reflecting Your love to those around me.

Thank You, Lord, for the gift of love. In the mighty and matchless name of Jesus, I pray, Amen.

Prayer 240: God's Assurance in Uncertainty

Scripture:

"The heart of man plans his way, but the Lord establishes his steps."

(Proverbs 16:9 ESV)

Prayer:

Father, I thank You for being in control of my life. While I may have my plans, I trust that You are establishing my steps. Help me to submit my desires to You and to seek Your guidance in every decision I make.

Lord, when I feel uncertain about the future, remind me that You are directing my path. Let me find peace in knowing that You are at work for my good.

Thank You, Lord, for establishing my steps. In the mighty and matchless name of Jesus, I pray, Amen.

Prayer 241: God's Healing in My Life

Scripture:

"He sent His word and healed them, and delivered them from their destructions."

(Psalm 107:20 NKJV)

Prayer:

Father, I thank You for the healing that comes through Your Word. I trust in Your ability to restore my health and spirit. Help me to seek Your truth in times of sickness and distress, believing in the power of Your promises.

Lord, when I or my loved ones are in need of healing, remind me to bring those needs before You. Let me hold onto the hope that Your Word brings comfort and restoration.

Thank You, Lord, for Your healing power in my life. In the mighty and matchless name of Jesus, I pray, Amen.

Prayer 242: God's Strength in Adversity

Scripture:

"I can do all things through Christ who strengthens me."
(Philippians 4:13 KJV)

Prayer:

Lord, I thank You for the strength You provide in every adversity. I know that I can overcome challenges because You empower me. Help me to rely on Your strength and to trust in Your ability to carry me through difficult times.

Father, when I feel weak or overwhelmed, remind me that I can do all things through You. Let me walk confidently, knowing that Your power is at work within me.

Thank You, Lord, for the strength that sustains me in my journey. In the mighty and matchless name of Jesus, I pray, Amen.

Prayer 243: God's Joy in My Heart

Scripture:

"The joy of the Lord is your strength."
(Nehemiah 8:10 KJV)

Prayer:

Father, I thank You for the joy that comes from knowing You. Your joy is my strength, and I choose to embrace it today. Help me to find joy in every circumstance, trusting that You are always with me.

Lord, when I feel weighed down by life's challenges, remind me of the joy You provide. Let Your joy uplift my spirit and enable me to face each day with hope.

Thank You, Lord, for the joy that fills my heart. In the mighty and matchless name of Jesus, I pray, Amen.

Prayer 244: God's Peace in My Life

Scripture:

"And let the peace of Christ rule in your hearts, to which indeed you were called in one body. And be thankful."
(Colossians 3:15 ESV)

Prayer:

Father, I thank You for the peace that comes from Christ. I desire for Your peace to rule in my heart, guiding my thoughts and actions. Help me to cultivate an attitude of gratitude, recognizing the blessings You provide.

Lord, when anxiety threatens to invade my heart, remind me to turn to You for peace. Let Your calming presence envelop me, allowing me to rest in Your assurance.

Thank You, Lord, for the peace that surpasses all understanding. In the mighty and matchless name of Jesus, I pray, Amen.

Prayer 245: God's Faithfulness Through Trials

Scripture:

"The Lord is good, a refuge in times of trouble. He cares for those who trust in Him."

(Nahum 1:7 NIV)

Prayer:

Father, I thank You for Your faithfulness during trials. You are a refuge in times of trouble, and I can always rely on Your care. Help me to trust in You, even when circumstances seem overwhelming.

Lord, when I feel lost in my struggles, remind me of Your promises. Let me find comfort and strength in knowing that You are my refuge and that You care deeply for me.

Thank You, Lord, for Your faithfulness through every challenge. In the mighty and matchless name of Jesus, I pray, Amen.

Prayer 246: God's Provision for My Needs

Scripture:

"But seek first the kingdom of God and His righteousness, and all these things will be added to you."
(Matthew 6:33 ESV)

Prayer:

Father, I thank You for the promise of provision. I choose to seek Your kingdom first, trusting that You will provide for all my needs. Help me to prioritize my relationship with You and to rely on Your faithfulness.

Lord, when I feel anxious about my needs or my future, remind me of Your past provision. Let me walk in faith, confident that You are taking care of me.

Thank You, Lord, for supplying all my needs. In the mighty and matchless name of Jesus, I pray, Amen.

Prayer 247: God's Assurance in My Life

Scripture:

"For I am with you, says the Lord, to save you; for I will make a full end of all the nations to which I have driven you, but I will not make a full end of you. I will chasten you in just measure, and I will not leave you altogether unpunished."

(Jeremiah 30:11 NKJV)

Prayer:

Father, I thank You for the assurance that You are always with me. In times of uncertainty and fear, I can find comfort in knowing that You are my Savior. Help me to trust in Your presence, especially when I face challenges.

Lord, when I feel overwhelmed or abandoned, remind me of Your promise to be with me. Let me rest in the truth that I am never alone, and that You are guiding me through every trial.

Thank You, Lord, for Your unwavering presence. In the mighty and matchless name of Jesus, I pray, Amen.

Prayer 248: God's Mercy in My Life

Scripture:

"The Lord is gracious and merciful; slow to anger and great in lovingkindness."

(Psalm 145:8 KJV)

Prayer:

Father, I thank You for Your mercy and grace that are new every morning. Your lovingkindness toward me is beyond measure, and I am so grateful for Your patience and compassion. Help me to extend that same grace to others in my life.

Lord, when I feel overwhelmed by guilt or shame, remind me of Your unfailing mercy. Let me walk in the freedom that comes from knowing I am forgiven.

Thank You, Lord, for Your abundant mercy. In the mighty and matchless name of Jesus, I pray, Amen.

Prayer 249: God's Light in My Darkness

Scripture:

"The people who walked in darkness have seen a great light; those who dwelt in a land of deep darkness, on them has light shone."

(Isaiah 9:2 ESV)

Prayer:

Father, I thank You for the light that shines in my darkness. In times of uncertainty and fear, I can find hope and guidance in You. Help me to seek Your light in every situation, trusting that it will illuminate my path.

Lord, when I feel surrounded by darkness, remind me that Your light dispels all shadows. Let me shine that light to others, sharing the hope that comes from knowing You.

Thank You, Lord, for being the light of my life. In the mighty and matchless name of Jesus, I pray, Amen.

Prayer 250: God's Assurance in All Circumstances

Scripture:

"And we know that in all things God works for the good of those who love Him, who have been called according to His purpose."

(Romans 8:28 NIV)

Prayer:

Father, I thank You for the assurance that You are working all things for my good. I trust that even in difficult times, You have a plan and purpose for my life. Help me to remember this truth when I face uncertainty.

Lord, when I feel overwhelmed by my circumstances, remind me that You are in control. Let me find comfort in knowing that You are always working for my benefit.

Thank You, Lord, for Your faithful assurance. In the mighty and matchless name of Jesus, I pray, Amen.

Prayer 251: God's Promise of Restoration

Scripture:

"I will restore to you the years that the locust has eaten."
(Joel 2:25 KJV)

Prayer:

Father, I thank You for Your promise of restoration. I trust that You can redeem the time that has been lost and bring healing to my heart. Help me to believe in Your ability to restore what has been broken in my life.

Lord, when I reflect on past losses, remind me that You are a God of renewal. Let me walk forward with hope, knowing that You are working to restore and renew.

Thank You, Lord, for Your promise of healing and restoration. In the mighty and matchless name of Jesus, I pray, Amen.

Prayer 252: God's Strength in Every Season

Scripture:

"Finally, be strong in the Lord and in the strength of His might."

(Ephesians 6:10 ESV)

Prayer:

Father, I thank You for the strength that comes from knowing You. I choose to lean on Your power in every season of my life. Help me to rely on Your strength rather than my own, especially when I feel weak or inadequate.

Lord, when I face challenges that seem overwhelming, remind me that I can draw strength from You. Let me stand firm, knowing that You are my source of power and resilience.

Thank You, Lord, for Your unwavering strength. In the mighty and matchless name of Jesus, I pray, Amen.

Prayer 253: God's Faithfulness in All Things

Scripture:

"The steadfast love of the Lord never ceases; His mercies never come to an end."

(Lamentations 3:22 ESV)

Prayer:

Father, I thank You for Your steadfast love that never fails. Your mercies are new every morning, and I am grateful for Your faithfulness. Help me to hold onto that truth during difficult times and to trust in Your goodness.

Lord, when I feel overwhelmed or discouraged, remind me of Your past faithfulness. Let me cling to the hope that You are always working for my good.

Thank You, Lord, for Your unchanging faithfulness. In the mighty and matchless name of Jesus, I pray, Amen.

Prayer 254: God's Comfort in Times of Grief

Scripture:

"He will wipe every tear from their eyes. There will be no more death or mourning or crying or pain, for the old order of things has passed away."

(Revelation 21:4 NIV)

Prayer:

Father, I thank You for the promise of comfort in my grief. You see my pain, and I trust that You will bring healing to my heart. Help me to seek Your comfort during these difficult times, knowing that You are always present.

Lord, when sorrow weighs heavily on my heart, remind me of the hope that lies ahead. Let me find solace in Your love, allowing Your presence to mend my brokenness.

Thank You, Lord, for being my comforter in times of grief. In the mighty and matchless name of Jesus, I pray, Amen.

Prayer 255: God's Peace in My Heart

Scripture:

"And the peace of God, which surpasses all understanding, will guard your hearts and your minds in Christ Jesus."
(Philippians 4:7 ESV)

Prayer:

Father, I thank You for the peace that comes from knowing You. I invite Your peace into my heart and mind, trusting that it will guard me against anxiety and fear. Help me to focus on You and Your promises.

Lord, when worries threaten to overwhelm me, remind me to turn to You for peace. Let Your calming presence fill my heart, allowing me to rest in Your assurance.

Thank You, Lord, for the peace that surpasses all understanding. In the mighty and matchless name of Jesus, I pray, Amen.

Prayer 256: God's Goodness in My Life

Scripture:

"Oh, taste and see that the Lord is good; blessed is the man who trusts in Him."

(Psalm 34:8 KJV)

Prayer:

Father, I thank You for Your goodness that is evident in my life. I want to experience the fullness of Your blessings and trust in Your faithful provision. Help me to see Your goodness in every circumstance.

Lord, when I feel discouraged, remind me of the many ways You have blessed me. Let my heart overflow with gratitude as I reflect on Your goodness.

Thank You, Lord, for the goodness that never fades. In the mighty and matchless name of Jesus, I pray, Amen.

Prayer 257: God's Light in My Darkness

Scripture:

"The Lord is my light and my salvation; whom shall I fear? The Lord is the stronghold of my life; of whom shall I be afraid?"

(Psalm 27:1 ESV)

Prayer:

Father, I thank You for being my light and salvation. You illuminate my path and protect me from harm. Help me to trust in You completely, knowing that I have nothing to fear.

Lord, when darkness surrounds me, remind me that Your light will guide me. Let me find comfort in Your presence, allowing Your truth to dispel any fears.

Thank You, Lord, for being my light and my stronghold. In the mighty and matchless name of Jesus, I pray, Amen.

Prayer 258: God's Guidance in My Life

Scripture:

"Trust in the Lord with all your heart, and do not lean on your own understanding."

(Proverbs 3:5 ESV)

Prayer:

Father, I thank You for the guidance You provide in my life. I choose to trust in You with my whole heart, knowing that Your ways are higher than mine. Help me to seek Your wisdom in every decision I make.

Lord, when I feel uncertain or confused, remind me to lean on Your understanding rather than my own. Let me walk in faith, trusting that You are directing my steps.

Thank You, Lord, for being my guide. In the mighty and matchless name of Jesus, I pray, Amen.

Prayer 259: God's Faithfulness in Every Situation

Scripture:

"The Lord is good, a stronghold in the day of trouble; He knows those who take refuge in Him."
(Nahum 1:7 ESV)

Prayer:

Father, I thank You for Your faithfulness that endures through every situation. You are a stronghold in my times of trouble, and I can always rely on You. Help me to find refuge in You when life gets challenging.

Lord, when I feel overwhelmed, remind me that You are my safe place. Let me lean on Your strength and find comfort in Your promises.

Thank You, Lord, for Your unwavering faithfulness. In the mighty and matchless name of Jesus, I pray, Amen.

Prayer 260: God's Hope for the Future

Scripture:

"For I know the plans I have for you, declares the Lord, plans to prosper you and not to harm you, plans to give you hope and a future."

(Jeremiah 29:11 NIV)

Prayer:

Father, I thank You for the hope You have promised for my future. I trust that Your plans are good and filled with purpose. Help me to seek Your will and to trust in Your timing, especially when I feel uncertain.

Lord, when I encounter obstacles, remind me that You have a plan for my life. Let me walk in faith, knowing that You are guiding me toward a bright future.

Thank You, Lord, for the hope and promise You have for me. In the mighty and matchless name of Jesus, I pray, Amen.

Prayer 261: God's Peace in Troubling Times

Scripture:

"You will keep him in perfect peace, whose mind is stayed on You, because he trusts in You."

(Isaiah 26:3 NKJV)

Prayer:

Father, I thank You for the promise of perfect peace. I choose to focus my mind on You and to trust in Your goodness. Help me to remain centered in Your presence, especially when the world around me feels chaotic.

Lord, when anxiety tries to take hold of my heart, remind me of Your unwavering peace. Let me rest in the assurance that You are in control, allowing Your peace to calm my spirit.

Thank You, Lord, for the perfect peace that comes from trusting You. In the mighty and matchless name of Jesus, I pray, Amen.

Prayer 262: God's Faithfulness in Every Challenge

Scripture:

"The Lord will fight for you, and you have only to be silent."
(Exodus 14:14 ESV)

Prayer:

Father, I thank You for Your promise to fight for me in every challenge I face. I can trust in Your strength and protection, knowing that You are always at work on my behalf. Help me to remain still and allow You to handle my battles.

Lord, when I feel overwhelmed by my circumstances, remind me that I don't have to fight alone. Let me find comfort in knowing that You are my defender and that You will work all things for my good.

Thank You, Lord, for Your faithfulness in every challenge. In the mighty and matchless name of Jesus, I pray, Amen.

Prayer 263: God's Comfort in My Weakness

Scripture:

"He gives power to the weak, and to those who have no might He increases strength."

(Isaiah 40:29 NKJV)

Prayer:

Father, I thank You for the strength You provide in my weakness. When I feel inadequate, I trust that Your power is made perfect in my limitations. Help me to rely on You fully, knowing that Your grace is sufficient for me.

Lord, when I face difficulties that seem overwhelming, remind me that I can find strength in You. Let me walk in confidence, trusting that You are my source of power.

Thank You, Lord, for Your comfort and strength in my weakness. In the mighty and matchless name of Jesus, I pray, Amen.

Prayer 264: God's Joy in My Life

Scripture:

"Rejoice in the Lord always; again I will say, rejoice."
(Philippians 4:4 ESV)

Prayer:

Father, I thank You for the joy that comes from knowing You. I choose to rejoice in You every day, regardless of my circumstances. Help me to cultivate a spirit of joy that reflects Your goodness in my life.

Lord, when I feel weighed down by challenges, remind me to focus on the blessings You have given. Let my heart be filled with joy, enabling me to share it with others.

Thank You, Lord, for the joy that sustains me. In the mighty and matchless name of Jesus, I pray, Amen.

Prayer 265: God's Provision in My Life

Scripture:

"And my God shall supply all your need according to His riches in glory by Christ Jesus."

> *(Philippians 4:19 NKJV)*

Prayer:

Father, I thank You for the promise of provision. You know my needs better than I do, and I trust that You will supply everything I require. Help me to rest in that promise and to seek You first in all things.

Lord, when I feel anxious about my needs or my future, remind me of Your past provision. Let me walk in faith, confident that You are taking care of me.

Thank You, Lord, for supplying all my needs. In the mighty and matchless name of Jesus, I pray, Amen.

Prayer 266: God's Assurance of His Love

Scripture:

"For I am convinced that neither death nor life, neither angels nor demons, neither the present nor the future, nor any powers, neither height nor depth, nor anything else in all creation, will be able to separate us from the love of God that is in Christ Jesus our Lord."

(Romans 8:38-39 NIV)

Prayer:

Father, I thank You for the assurance that nothing can separate me from Your love. Your love is unchanging and everlasting, and I am grateful for that truth. Help me to fully embrace Your love and to share it with others.

Lord, when I feel unworthy or distant, remind me of the depth of Your love. Let me rest in the assurance that I am forever loved and accepted by You.

Thank You, Lord, for Your everlasting love. In the mighty and matchless name of Jesus, I pray, Amen.

Prayer 267: God's Light in My Life

Scripture:

"The Lord is my light and my salvation; whom shall I fear? The Lord is the stronghold of my life; of whom shall I be afraid?"

(Psalm 27:1 ESV)

Prayer:

Father, I thank You for being my light and salvation. You illuminate my path and protect me from harm. Help me to trust in You completely, knowing that I have nothing to fear.

Lord, when darkness surrounds me, remind me that Your light dispels all shadows. Let me walk confidently in Your truth, shining Your light to others in need.

Thank You, Lord, for being my light and my stronghold. In the mighty and matchless name of Jesus, I pray, Amen.

Prayer 268: God's Comfort in Times of Sorrow

Scripture:

"Cast all your anxiety on Him because He cares for you."
(1 Peter 5:7 NIV)

Prayer:

Father, I thank You for the comfort that comes from casting my cares on You. You understand my pain and heartache, and I trust that You will bring healing to my wounds. Help me to lean on You during my times of sorrow.

Lord, when I feel overwhelmed by grief, remind me that You are my refuge. Let Your love surround me, bringing peace and comfort to my heart.

Thank You, Lord, for being my source of comfort in times of sorrow. In the mighty and matchless name of Jesus, I pray, Amen.

Prayer 269: God's Wisdom in My Decisions

Scripture:

"If any of you lacks wisdom, let him ask of God, who gives to all liberally and without reproach, and it will be given to him."

(James 1:5 NKJV)

Prayer:

Father, I thank You for the gift of wisdom that comes from You. I ask for Your guidance in every decision I make, trusting that You will provide the understanding I need. Help me to seek You first in all things.

Lord, when I feel uncertain or confused, remind me to turn to Your Word for guidance. Let Your wisdom illuminate my path, leading me toward what is best.

Thank You, Lord, for being my source of wisdom. In the mighty and matchless name of Jesus, I pray, Amen.

Prayer 270: God's Hope for the Future

Scripture:

"For I know the plans I have for you, declares the Lord, plans to prosper you and not to harm you, plans to give you hope and a future."

(Jeremiah 29:11 NIV)

Prayer:

Father, I thank You for the hope You have promised for my future. I trust that Your plans are good and filled with purpose. Help me to seek Your will and to trust in Your timing, especially when I feel uncertain.

Lord, when I encounter obstacles, remind me that You have a plan for my life. Let me walk in faith, knowing that You are guiding me toward a bright future.

Thank You, Lord, for the hope and promise You have for me. In the mighty and matchless name of Jesus, I pray, Amen.

Prayer 271: God's Assurance in Difficult Times

Scripture:

"When you pass through the waters, I will be with you; and through the rivers, they shall not overflow you."
(Isaiah 43:2 NKJV)

Prayer:

Father, I thank You for Your assurance that You are always with me, especially during difficult times. When I face challenges that seem overwhelming, I trust that You will protect and guide me through them. Help me to lean on You and to find comfort in Your presence.

Lord, when the storms of life threaten to overwhelm me, remind me of Your promise. Let me walk in faith, knowing that You are by my side, bringing peace and safety.

Thank You, Lord, for being my constant companion. In the mighty and matchless name of Jesus, I pray, Amen.

Prayer 272: God's Healing Presence

Scripture:

"But He was pierced for our transgressions; He was crushed for our iniquities; the punishment that brought us peace was on Him, and by His wounds we are healed."
(Isaiah 53:5 NIV)

Prayer:

Father, I thank You for the healing that comes through Jesus. I believe in the power of His wounds to bring restoration and wholeness. Help me to bring my pain and struggles to You, trusting in Your healing presence.

Lord, when I feel broken or unwell, remind me that Your healing is available. Let me rest in the assurance that You are actively restoring me, both physically and spiritually.

Thank You, Lord, for Your healing touch in my life. In the mighty and matchless name of Jesus, I pray, Amen.

Prayer 273: God's Light in Darkness

Scripture:

"The light shines in the darkness, and the darkness has not overcome it."

(John 1:5 ESV)

Prayer:

Father, I thank You for the light that shines in my life. Even when darkness surrounds me, I know that Your light cannot be extinguished. Help me to seek Your light and to reflect it to others in need.

Lord, when I feel lost or overwhelmed by fear, remind me of the hope that Your light brings. Let me walk in confidence, knowing that You are my guiding light.

Thank You, Lord, for illuminating my path. In the mighty and matchless name of Jesus, I pray, Amen.

Prayer 274: God's Faithfulness in Every Season

Scripture:

"Jesus Christ is the same yesterday, today, and forever."
(Hebrews 13:8 ESV)

Prayer:

Father, I thank You for Your unchanging faithfulness. You are the same in every season of my life, and I can always count on You. Help me to remember this truth when life feels uncertain or challenging.

Lord, when I face trials, remind me that You are with me, guiding and providing every step of the way. Let me find comfort in the knowledge that Your faithfulness endures forever.

Thank You, Lord, for Your steadfastness in my life. In the mighty and matchless name of Jesus, I pray, Amen.

Prayer 275: God's Love in My Life

Scripture:

"For God so loved the world that He gave His one and only Son, that whoever believes in Him shall not perish but have eternal life."

(John 3:16 NIV)

Prayer:

Father, I thank You for the incredible love You have shown me through Jesus. Your sacrifice brings me hope and salvation. Help me to fully understand the depth of Your love and to share that love with those around me.

Lord, when I feel unworthy or disconnected, remind me of the truth of Your love. Let me rest in the assurance that I am cherished and accepted by You.

Thank You, Lord, for Your everlasting love. In the mighty and matchless name of Jesus, I pray, Amen.

Prayer 276: God's Purpose in My Journey

Scripture:

"For we are His workmanship, created in Christ Jesus for good works, which God prepared beforehand that we should walk in them."

(Ephesians 2:10 ESV)

Prayer:

Father, I thank You for the unique purpose You have for my life. I am Your creation, designed for good works. Help me to seek Your will and to walk in the path You have laid out for me.

Lord, when I feel lost or uncertain about my direction, remind me that You have a plan for my life. Let me embrace my purpose and walk in faith, trusting that You are leading me.

Thank You, Lord, for the purpose You have instilled in me. In the mighty and matchless name of Jesus, I pray, Amen.

Prayer 277: God's Strength in My Weakness

Scripture:

"But He said to me, 'My grace is sufficient for you, for My power is made perfect in weakness.'"

(2 Corinthians 12:9 NKJV)

Prayer:

Father, I thank You for Your grace that is sufficient for every need. In my weaknesses, I find strength in You. Help me to embrace my limitations and rely on Your power to guide me through.

Lord, when I feel overwhelmed or inadequate, remind me that Your strength is made perfect in my weakness. Let me walk in confidence, knowing that I am empowered by Your grace.

Thank You, Lord, for Your sufficient grace in my life. In the mighty and matchless name of Jesus, I pray, Amen.

Prayer 278: God's Hope in Troubling Times

Scripture:

"The Lord is good to those who wait for Him, to the soul who seeks Him."

(Lamentations 3:25 ESV)

Prayer:

Father, I thank You for the hope that comes from waiting on You. I trust that You are working all things for my good, even when I cannot see the outcome. Help me to seek You diligently and to wait patiently for Your perfect timing.

Lord, when I feel impatient or anxious, remind me to turn to You for strength. Let my heart be filled with hope as I wait on Your promises.

Thank You, Lord, for the hope that sustains me. In the mighty and matchless name of Jesus, I pray, Amen.

Prayer 279: God's Assurance of His Presence

Scripture:

"Fear not, for I am with you; be not dismayed, for I am your God; I will strengthen you, I will help you, I will uphold you with My righteous right hand."

(Isaiah 41:10 ESV)

Prayer:

Father, I thank You for the assurance that You are always with me. In times of fear and uncertainty, I can find strength in Your presence. Help me to trust in Your guidance and support as I face life's challenges.

Lord, when I feel anxious or afraid, remind me of Your promises. Let me find comfort in knowing that You are my God and that You will uphold me.

Thank You, Lord, for being my constant companion. In the mighty and matchless name of Jesus, I pray, Amen.

Prayer 280: God's Love and Kindness

Scripture:

"But the fruit of the Spirit is love, joy, peace, forbearance, kindness, goodness, faithfulness, gentleness, and self-control."

(Galatians 5:22-23 NIV)

Prayer:

Father, I thank You for the gift of the Holy Spirit and the fruit that comes from knowing You. Help me to cultivate love, kindness, and goodness in my life, reflecting Your character in my interactions with others.

Lord, when I encounter challenges or difficult people, remind me to respond with kindness and grace. Let me be a vessel of Your love, sharing Your goodness with those around me.

Thank You, Lord, for the fruit of the Spirit that enriches my life. In the mighty and matchless name of Jesus, I pray, Amen.

Prayer 281: God's Strength in My Weakness

Scripture:

"Therefore I take pleasure in infirmities, in reproaches, in needs, in persecutions, in distresses, for Christ's sake. For when I am weak, then I am strong."

(2 Corinthians 12:10 NKJV)

Prayer:

Father, I thank You for the strength that arises in my weakness. It is in those moments of vulnerability that I experience Your power most profoundly. Help me to embrace my limitations and to lean into Your strength.

Lord, when I face difficulties that seem insurmountable, remind me that Your grace is sufficient for me. Let my weaknesses become opportunities for Your strength to shine through.

Thank You, Lord, for Your strength that sustains me in my times of need. In the mighty and matchless name of Jesus, I pray, Amen.

Prayer 282: God's Goodness in Every Situation

Scripture:

"Oh, give thanks to the Lord, for He is good! For His mercy endures forever."
(Psalm 136:1 NKJV)

Prayer:

Father, I thank You for Your goodness that is evident in every situation. Your mercy never fails, and I am grateful for Your faithfulness. Help me to cultivate a heart of gratitude, recognizing Your blessings in my life.

Lord, when I feel discouraged, remind me of the countless ways You have shown Your goodness. Let my heart overflow with thankfulness, and may I share that gratitude with others.

Thank You, Lord, for Your goodness that sustains me. In the mighty and matchless name of Jesus, I pray, Amen.

Prayer 283: God's Presence in Every Storm

Scripture:

"And He awoke and rebuked the wind and said to the sea, 'Peace! Be still!' And the wind ceased, and there was a great calm."

(Mark 4:39 ESV)

Prayer:

Father, I thank You for the authority You have over every storm in my life. I trust that even when chaos surrounds me, You can bring peace and calm to my situation. Help me to rest in Your presence, knowing that You are in control.

Lord, when I feel anxious or overwhelmed, remind me to call on You. Let me find comfort in Your ability to still the storms and provide calmness in my heart.

Thank You, Lord, for Your peace that surpasses all understanding. In the mighty and matchless name of Jesus, I pray, Amen.

Prayer 284: God's Faithfulness in Every Trial

Scripture:

"Many are the afflictions of the righteous, but the Lord delivers him out of them all."

(Psalm 34:19 NKJV)

Prayer:

Father, I thank You for Your faithfulness during trials. Even when I face afflictions, I trust in Your promise to deliver me. Help me to remain steadfast in my faith, knowing that You are always at work for my good.

Lord, when I feel overwhelmed by my struggles, remind me of Your past deliverances. Let my faith be strengthened as I look back on how You have always been there for me.

Thank You, Lord, for Your unwavering faithfulness through every trial. In the mighty and matchless name of Jesus, I pray, Amen.

Prayer 285: God's Love in My Life

Scripture:

"But God, who is rich in mercy, because of His great love with which He loved us."

(Ephesians 2:4 NKJV)

Prayer:

Father, I thank You for Your great love and mercy. You have poured out Your love into my life, and I am forever grateful for that. Help me to fully embrace Your love and to share it with those around me.

Lord, when I struggle with feelings of unworthiness, remind me of the depth of Your love. Let me rest in the assurance that I am cherished and accepted by You, no matter my circumstances.

Thank You, Lord, for Your everlasting love. In the mighty and matchless name of Jesus, I pray, Amen.

Prayer 286: God's Wisdom in My Decisions

Scripture:

"For the Lord gives wisdom; from His mouth come knowledge and understanding."

(Proverbs 2:6 ESV)

Prayer:

Father, I thank You for the wisdom that comes from You. I ask for Your guidance in every decision I face, trusting that You will provide the understanding I need. Help me to seek Your wisdom in all areas of my life.

Lord, when I feel uncertain or confused, remind me to turn to Your Word for clarity. Let Your wisdom illuminate my path and help me make choices that honor You.

Thank You, Lord, for being my source of wisdom. In the mighty and matchless name of Jesus, I pray, Amen.

Prayer 287: God's Assurance of His Presence

Scripture:

"The Lord your God is in your midst, a mighty one who will save; He will rejoice over you with gladness; He will quiet you by His love; He will exult over you with loud singing."
(Zephaniah 3:17 ESV)

Prayer:

Father, I thank You for the assurance of Your presence in my life. You are my mighty Savior, and I find comfort in knowing that You rejoice over me. Help me to be aware of Your loving presence, especially during challenging times.

Lord, when I feel anxious or alone, remind me that You are always near. Let me find peace in the knowledge that You are celebrating and caring for me.

Thank You, Lord, for Your comforting presence. In the mighty and matchless name of Jesus, I pray, Amen.

Prayer 288: God's Peace in My Heart

Scripture:

"Let not your hearts be troubled, neither let them be afraid."
(John 14:27 ESV)

Prayer:

Father, I thank You for the peace that comes from knowing You. I choose to cast aside my fears and anxieties, trusting that You are in control of my life. Help me to hold onto Your peace in every situation.

Lord, when troubling thoughts arise, remind me to focus on You. Let Your peace fill my heart and mind, calming the storms that threaten my joy.

Thank You, Lord, for the peace that surpasses all understanding. In the mighty and matchless name of Jesus, I pray, Amen.

Prayer 289: God's Guidance in My Journey

Scripture:

"In all your ways acknowledge Him, and He will make straight your paths."

(Proverbs 3:6 ESV)

Prayer:

Father, I thank You for the guidance You provide in my life. I desire to acknowledge You in all my ways, trusting that You will lead me on the right path. Help me to seek Your will in every decision I make.

Lord, when I feel lost or uncertain, remind me to turn to You for direction. Let me walk in faith, knowing that You are establishing my steps.

Thank You, Lord, for being my guide. In the mighty and matchless name of Jesus, I pray, Amen.

Prayer 290: God's Strength in Adversity

Scripture:

"But He said to me, 'My grace is sufficient for you, for My power is made perfect in weakness.' Therefore I will boast all the more gladly about my weaknesses, so that Christ's power may rest on me."

(2 Corinthians 12:9 NIV)

Prayer:

Father, I thank You for Your grace that is sufficient for every need. In my weaknesses, I find strength in You. Help me to embrace my limitations and rely on Your power to guide me through.

Lord, when I feel overwhelmed or inadequate, remind me that Your strength is made perfect in my weakness. Let me walk in confidence, knowing that I am empowered by Your grace.

Thank You, Lord, for Your sufficient grace in my life. In the mighty and matchless name of Jesus, I pray, Amen.

Prayer 291: God's Assurance of His Guidance

Scripture:

"The Lord will guide you continually, and satisfy your desire in scorched places, and make your bones strong."
(Isaiah 58:11 ESV)

Prayer:

Father, I thank You for the assurance that You will guide me continually. In times of uncertainty, I trust that You will lead me and provide for my needs. Help me to rely on Your guidance as I navigate the challenges of life.

Lord, when I feel lost or in need of direction, remind me to seek You first. Let me find comfort in knowing that You are always with me, ready to guide my steps.

Thank You, Lord, for being my constant guide. In the mighty and matchless name of Jesus, I pray, Amen.

Prayer 292: God's Comfort in Grief

Scripture:

"Blessed are those who mourn, for they shall be comforted."
(Matthew 5:4 ESV)

Prayer:

Father, I thank You for the promise of comfort for those who mourn. You understand my pain, and I trust that You will bring healing to my heart. Help me to seek Your comfort during this time of sorrow, knowing that You are always present.

Lord, when grief feels overwhelming, remind me of Your love and compassion. Let me find solace in Your presence, allowing Your comfort to fill my heart and restore my spirit.

Thank You, Lord, for being my comforter in times of grief. In the mighty and matchless name of Jesus, I pray, Amen.

Prayer 293: God's Faithfulness in Every Season

Scripture:

"The steadfast love of the Lord never ceases; His mercies never come to an end; they are new every morning; great is Your faithfulness."

(Lamentations 3:22-23 ESV)

Prayer:

Father, I thank You for Your steadfast love and mercy that are new every morning. I am grateful for Your faithfulness that sustains me through every season of life. Help me to wake up with a heart full of gratitude, ready to embrace the new day You have given.

Lord, when I feel discouraged or overwhelmed, remind me of Your past faithfulness. Let me cling to the truth that You are always working for my good.

Thank You, Lord, for Your unwavering faithfulness. In the mighty and matchless name of Jesus, I pray, Amen.

Prayer 294: God's Joy in My Heart

Scripture:

"You make known to me the path of life; in Your presence there is fullness of joy; at Your right hand are pleasures forevermore."

(Psalm 16:11 ESV)

Prayer:

Father, I thank You for the joy that comes from being in Your presence. I desire to experience the fullness of joy that only You can provide. Help me to seek You daily, knowing that true joy is found in communion with You.

Lord, when life's challenges threaten to steal my joy, remind me to turn to You. Let me find strength in Your presence and share that joy with others.

Thank You, Lord, for the joy that fills my heart. In the mighty and matchless name of Jesus, I pray, Amen.

Prayer 295: God's Protection Over My Life

Scripture:

"The Lord is my shepherd; I shall not want. He makes me lie down in green pastures. He leads me beside still waters."
(Psalm 23:1-2 ESV)

Prayer:

Father, I thank You for being my Shepherd. You guide and protect me, ensuring that I lack nothing. Help me to trust in Your care, knowing that You lead me to places of peace and rest.

Lord, when I feel anxious or afraid, remind me that You are my protector. Let me find comfort in the knowledge that I am safe in Your arms.

Thank You, Lord, for Your protection that surrounds me. In the mighty and matchless name of Jesus, I pray, Amen.

Prayer 296: God's Assurance of His Love

Scripture:

"For I am convinced that neither death nor life, neither angels nor demons, neither the present nor the future, nor any powers, neither height nor depth, nor anything else in all creation, will be able to separate us from the love of God that is in Christ Jesus our Lord."

(Romans 8:38-39 NIV)

Prayer:

Father, I thank You for the assurance that nothing can separate me from Your love. Your love is unchanging and everlasting, and I am grateful for that truth. Help me to fully embrace Your love and to share it with others.

Lord, when I feel unworthy or distant, remind me of the depth of Your love. Let me rest in the assurance that I am forever loved and accepted by You.

Thank You, Lord, for Your everlasting love. In the mighty and matchless name of Jesus, I pray, Amen.

Prayer 297: God's Goodness in My Life

Scripture:

"Oh, give thanks to the Lord, for He is good! For His mercy endures forever."

(Psalm 136:1 NKJV)

Prayer:

Father, I thank You for Your goodness that is evident in my life. I want to experience the fullness of Your blessings and trust in Your faithful provision. Help me to see Your goodness in every situation.

Lord, when I feel discouraged, remind me of the countless ways You have blessed me. Let my heart overflow with gratitude as I reflect on Your goodness.

Thank You, Lord, for the goodness that never fades. In the mighty and matchless name of Jesus, I pray, Amen.

Prayer 298: God's Peace in My Heart

Scripture:

"The peace of God, which surpasses all understanding, will guard your hearts and your minds in Christ Jesus."
(Philippians 4:7 ESV)

Prayer:

Father, I thank You for the peace that comes from knowing You. I invite Your peace into my heart and mind, trusting that it will guard me against anxiety and fear. Help me to hold onto Your peace in every situation.

Lord, when troubling thoughts arise, remind me to focus on You. Let Your calming presence fill me, allowing me to rest in Your assurance.

Thank You, Lord, for the peace that surpasses all understanding. In the mighty and matchless name of Jesus, I pray, Amen.

Prayer 299: God's Wisdom in My Decisions

Scripture:

"If any of you lacks wisdom, let him ask of God, who gives to all liberally and without reproach, and it will be given to him."

(James 1:5 NKJV)

Prayer:

Father, I thank You for the gift of wisdom that comes from You. I ask for Your guidance in every decision I make, trusting that You will provide the understanding I need. Help me to seek You first in all things.

Lord, when I feel uncertain or confused, remind me to turn to Your Word for guidance. Let Your wisdom illuminate my path, leading me toward what is best.

Thank You, Lord, for being my source of wisdom. In the mighty and matchless name of Jesus, I pray, Amen.

Prayer 300: God's Faithfulness in Every Season

Scripture:

"The steadfast love of the Lord never ceases; His mercies never come to an end; they are new every morning; great is Your faithfulness."

(Lamentations 3:22-23 ESV)

Prayer:

Father, I thank You for Your steadfast love and mercies that are new every morning. I am grateful for Your faithfulness that sustains me through every season of life. Help me to wake up with a heart full of gratitude, ready to embrace the new day You have given.

Lord, when I feel discouraged or overwhelmed, remind me of Your past faithfulness. Let me cling to the truth that You are always working for my good.

Thank You, Lord, for Your unwavering faithfulness. In the mighty and matchless name of Jesus, I pray, Amen.

Prayer 301: God's Comfort in Times of Distress

Scripture:

"The Lord is close to the brokenhearted and saves those who are crushed in spirit."
(Psalm 34:18 NIV)

Prayer:

Father, I thank You for Your closeness in times of distress. You understand my pain, and I trust that You will bring healing to my heart. Help me to lean on You when I feel broken and in need of comfort.

Lord, when life's burdens feel too heavy, remind me that You are near. Let me find solace in Your presence, allowing Your love to mend my wounds and restore my spirit.

Thank You, Lord, for being my comforter in times of need. In the mighty and matchless name of Jesus, I pray, Amen.

Prayer 302: God's Assurance of His Promises

Scripture:

"For all the promises of God find their Yes in Him. That is why it is through Him that we utter our Amen to God for His glory."

(2 Corinthians 1:20 ESV)

Prayer:

Father, I thank You for the assurance that all Your promises are fulfilled in Christ. I trust that Your Word is true and that You are faithful to keep Your promises. Help me to remain steadfast in faith as I wait for Your promises to come to fruition.

Lord, when doubt creeps in, remind me of Your past faithfulness. Let me hold onto the truth that You are always working for my good and glory.

Thank You, Lord, for Your unwavering promises. In the mighty and matchless name of Jesus, I pray, Amen.

Prayer 303: God's Healing in My Life

Scripture:

"He heals the brokenhearted and binds up their wounds."
(Psalm 147:3 ESV)

Prayer:

Father, I thank You for Your healing touch in my life. You see my pain and brokenness, and I trust in Your ability to restore my heart. Help me to bring my wounds to You, knowing that You care deeply for me.

Lord, when I feel overwhelmed by grief or hurt, remind me of Your promise to heal. Let Your loving presence bring comfort and restoration to every area of my life.

Thank You, Lord, for Your compassionate healing. In the mighty and matchless name of Jesus, I pray, Amen.

Prayer 304: God's Joy in My Life

Scripture:

"The joy of the Lord is your strength."
                    (Nehemiah 8:10 KJV)

Prayer:

Father, I thank You for the joy that comes from knowing You. Your joy is my strength, and I choose to embrace it today. Help me to find joy in every circumstance, trusting that You are always with me.

Lord, when I feel weighed down by life's challenges, remind me of the joy You provide. Let Your joy uplift my spirit and enable me to face each day with hope.

Thank You, Lord, for the joy that fills my heart. In the mighty and matchless name of Jesus, I pray, Amen.

Prayer 305: God's Faithfulness in My Journey

Scripture:

"The Lord your God is with you, the Mighty Warrior who saves. He will take great delight in you; in His love, He will no longer rebuke you, but will rejoice over you with singing."

(Zephaniah 3:17 NIV)

Prayer:

Father, I thank You for Your faithfulness throughout my journey. You are the Mighty Warrior who saves, and I can take delight in Your love. Help me to trust in Your guidance as I walk the path You have laid out for me.

Lord, when I encounter difficulties, remind me of Your promises. Let me find comfort in knowing that You delight in me and rejoice over my life.

Thank You, Lord, for being my faithful companion. In the mighty and matchless name of Jesus, I pray, Amen.

Prayer 306: God's Strength in My Challenges

Scripture:

"I can do all things through Christ who strengthens me."
(Philippians 4:13 NKJV)

Prayer:

Father, I thank You for the strength You provide in every challenge I face. I trust that I can overcome obstacles because You empower me. Help me to rely on Your strength and to walk confidently in faith.

Lord, when I feel weak or unable to continue, remind me that I can do all things through You. Let me find courage in Your presence and the assurance that You are with me.

Thank You, Lord, for the strength that sustains me. In the mighty and matchless name of Jesus, I pray, Amen.

Prayer 307: God's Wisdom in My Decisions

Scripture:

"If any of you lacks wisdom, let him ask of God, who gives to all liberally and without reproach, and it will be given to him."

(James 1:5 NKJV)

Prayer:

Father, I thank You for the wisdom that comes from You. I seek Your guidance in every decision I make, trusting that You will provide the understanding I need. Help me to seek You first and rely on Your insight.

Lord, when I feel uncertain or confused, remind me to turn to Your Word for direction. Let Your wisdom illuminate my path, leading me toward what is best.

Thank You, Lord, for being my source of wisdom. In the mighty and matchless name of Jesus, I pray, Amen.

Prayer 308: God's Promise of Hope

Scripture:

"The Lord is good to those who wait for Him, to the soul who seeks Him."

(Lamentations 3:25 ESV)

Prayer:

Father, I thank You for the hope that comes from waiting on You. I trust that You are working all things for my good, even when I cannot see the outcome. Help me to seek You diligently and to wait patiently for Your perfect timing.

Lord, when I feel impatient or anxious, remind me to turn to You for strength. Let my heart be filled with hope as I wait on Your promises.

Thank You, Lord, for the hope that sustains me. In the mighty and matchless name of Jesus, I pray, Amen.

Prayer 309: God's Comfort in My Life

Scripture:

"Cast all your anxiety on Him because He cares for you."
(1 Peter 5:7 NIV)

Prayer:

Father, I thank You for the comfort that comes from casting my cares on You. You understand my pain and heartache, and I trust that You will bring healing to my wounds. Help me to lean on You during my times of distress.

Lord, when I feel burdened by anxiety, remind me to turn to You for comfort. Let Your loving presence envelop me, bringing peace and restoration to my spirit.

Thank You, Lord, for being my source of comfort. In the mighty and matchless name of Jesus, I pray, Amen.

Prayer 310: God's Guidance in My Journey

Scripture:

"In all your ways acknowledge Him, and He will make straight your paths."

(Proverbs 3:6 ESV)

Prayer:

Father, I thank You for Your guidance in my life. I desire to acknowledge You in all my ways, trusting that You will lead me on the right path. Help me to seek Your will in every decision I make.

Lord, when I feel lost or uncertain, remind me to turn to You for direction. Let me walk in faith, knowing that You are establishing my steps.

Thank You, Lord, for being my guide. In the mighty and matchless name of Jesus, I pray, Amen.

Prayer 311: God's Restoration in My Life

Scripture:

"And I will restore to you the years that the swarming locust has eaten."

(Joel 2:25 KJV)

Prayer:

Father, I thank You for Your promise of restoration. No matter what has been lost, I trust that You can bring healing and renewal into my life. Help me to hold onto hope as I wait for the restoration You have promised.

Lord, when I look back on my past losses, remind me that You are a God who redeems and restores. Let me walk forward with confidence, anticipating the healing You will bring.

Thank You, Lord, for Your faithfulness in restoring my life. In the mighty and matchless name of Jesus, I pray, Amen.

Prayer 312: God's Faithfulness Through Trials

Scripture:

"The Lord is good, a stronghold in the day of trouble; He knows those who trust in Him."
(Nahum 1:7 NKJV)

Prayer:

Father, I thank You for Your faithfulness during trials. You are my stronghold in times of trouble, and I can always rely on You. Help me to trust in You fully, even when circumstances are challenging.

Lord, when I feel overwhelmed, remind me that You are my refuge and strength. Let me find comfort in Your presence, knowing that You are always there to support me.

Thank You, Lord, for being my faithful companion. In the mighty and matchless name of Jesus, I pray, Amen.

Prayer 313: God's Joy in My Life

Scripture:

"Rejoice in the Lord always; again I will say, rejoice."
(Philippians 4:4 ESV)

Prayer:

Father, I thank You for the joy that comes from knowing You. I choose to rejoice in You daily, regardless of my circumstances. Help me to find joy in every moment, trusting that You are with me.

Lord, when life's challenges try to steal my joy, remind me of the blessings You have provided. Let my heart overflow with gratitude and joy as I reflect on Your goodness.

Thank You, Lord, for the joy that fills my heart. In the mighty and matchless name of Jesus, I pray, Amen.

Prayer 314: God's Peace in My Heart

Scripture:

"Let not your heart be troubled, neither let it be afraid."
(John 14:27 KJV)

Prayer:

Father, I thank You for the peace that comes from knowing You. I choose to cast aside my fears and anxieties, trusting that You are in control. Help me to hold onto Your peace in every situation.

Lord, when troubling thoughts arise, remind me to focus on Your promises. Let Your calming presence fill my heart, allowing me to rest in Your assurance.

Thank You, Lord, for the peace that surpasses all understanding. In the mighty and matchless name of Jesus, I pray, Amen.

Prayer 315: God's Strength in My Weakness

Scripture:

"He gives power to the weak, and to those who have no might He increases strength."
$$\text{(Isaiah 40:29 NKJV)}$$

Prayer:

Father, I thank You for being my source of strength. In my weaknesses, I find Your power, and I trust that You will carry me through. Help me to embrace my limitations and rely on Your strength.

Lord, when I feel overwhelmed, remind me that Your grace is sufficient. Let me walk in confidence, knowing that Your strength is made perfect in my weakness.

Thank You, Lord, for Your strength that sustains me. In the mighty and matchless name of Jesus, I pray, Amen.

Prayer 316: God's Goodness in My Life

Scripture:

"Oh, taste and see that the Lord is good; blessed is the man who trusts in Him."

(Psalm 34:8 KJV)

Prayer:

Father, I thank You for Your goodness that is evident in my life. I want to experience the fullness of Your blessings and trust in Your faithful provision. Help me to see Your goodness in every situation.

Lord, when I feel discouraged, remind me of the countless ways You have shown Your goodness. Let my heart overflow with gratitude as I reflect on Your faithfulness.

Thank You, Lord, for Your goodness that never fades. In the mighty and matchless name of Jesus, I pray, Amen.

Prayer 317: God's Faithfulness in Every Season

Scripture:

"The steadfast love of the Lord never ceases; His mercies never come to an end."
(Lamentations 3:22 NKJV)

Prayer:

Father, I thank You for Your steadfast love and mercies that are new every morning. Your faithfulness sustains me through every season of life. Help me to wake up each day with a heart full of gratitude.

Lord, when I feel overwhelmed or discouraged, remind me of Your past faithfulness. Let me cling to the truth that You are always working for my good.

Thank You, Lord, for Your unwavering faithfulness. In the mighty and matchless name of Jesus, I pray, Amen.

Prayer 318: God's Hope for the Future

Scripture:

"For I know the thoughts that I think toward you, says the Lord, thoughts of peace and not of evil, to give you a future and a hope."

(Jeremiah 29:11 KJV)

Prayer:

Father, I thank You for the hope You have promised for my future. I trust that Your plans are good and filled with purpose. Help me to seek Your will and to trust in Your timing.

Lord, when I feel anxious about my future, remind me that You are in control. Let me walk in faith, knowing that You are guiding me toward a bright future.

Thank You, Lord, for the hope and promise You have for me. In the mighty and matchless name of Jesus, I pray, Amen.

Prayer 319: God's Assurance of His Presence

Scripture:

"Fear not, for I am with you; be not dismayed, for I am your God; I will strengthen you, I will help you, I will uphold you with My righteous right hand."
(Isaiah 41:10 NKJV)

Prayer:

Father, I thank You for the assurance that You are always with me. In times of fear and uncertainty, I can find strength in Your presence. Help me to trust in Your guidance as I face life's challenges.

Lord, when I feel anxious or alone, remind me of Your promises. Let me find comfort in knowing that You are my God and that You will uphold me.

Thank You, Lord, for being my constant companion. In the mighty and matchless name of Jesus, I pray, Amen.

Prayer 320: God's Love in My Life

Scripture:

"But God demonstrates His own love toward us, in that while we were still sinners, Christ died for us."
                    (Romans 5:8 NKJV)

Prayer:

Father, I thank You for the incredible love You have shown me through Christ. Your love is unconditional and sacrificial, and I am forever grateful for that assurance. Help me to fully grasp the depth of that love and to share it with others.

Lord, when I feel unworthy or distant, remind me of the depth of Your love. Let me rest in the assurance that I am loved and accepted by You.

Thank You, Lord, for Your everlasting love. In the mighty and matchless name of Jesus, I pray, Amen.

Prayer 321: God's Guidance in My Life

Scripture:

"I will instruct you and teach you in the way you should go; I will guide you with My eye."

(Psalm 32:8 NKJV)

Prayer:

Father, I thank You for the promise of Your guidance in my life. You have promised to instruct and teach me, and I trust that You will lead me on the right path. Help me to be attentive to Your voice and to follow Your direction.

Lord, when I feel lost or uncertain about my decisions, remind me to seek You first. Let Your wisdom illuminate my path, guiding me toward what is best.

Thank You, Lord, for being my guide. In the mighty and matchless name of Jesus, I pray, Amen.

Prayer 322: God's Peace in Every Situation

Scripture:

"And let the peace of Christ rule in your hearts, to which indeed you were called in one body. And be thankful."
(Colossians 3:15 ESV)

Prayer:

Father, I thank You for the peace that comes from knowing You. I desire for Your peace to rule in my heart, guiding my thoughts and actions. Help me to cultivate an attitude of gratitude, recognizing the blessings You provide.

Lord, when I face challenges that threaten my peace, remind me to turn to You. Let Your peace fill my heart and mind, calming my spirit and allowing me to rest in Your presence.

Thank You, Lord, for the peace that sustains me. In the mighty and matchless name of Jesus, I pray, Amen.

Prayer 323: God's Strength in Adversity

Scripture:

"Be strong, and let your heart take courage, all you who wait for the Lord!"
(Psalm 31:24 ESV)

Prayer:

Father, I thank You for the strength You provide in adversity. I trust that You will give me the courage to face every challenge. Help me to be strong and to wait patiently for Your deliverance.

Lord, when I feel weak or overwhelmed, remind me that my strength comes from You. Let me find courage in Your presence and be steadfast in my faith.

Thank You, Lord, for being my source of strength. In the mighty and matchless name of Jesus, I pray, Amen.

Prayer 324: God's Promise of Restoration

Scripture:

"He will restore the years that the swarming locust has eaten."

(Joel 2:25 KJV)

Prayer:

Father, I thank You for Your promise of restoration. You are able to bring healing and renewal to every area of my life. Help me to believe in Your power to restore what has been lost.

Lord, when I reflect on my past, remind me that You are a God who redeems and restores. Let me walk forward with hope, anticipating the restoration You have promised.

Thank You, Lord, for Your faithfulness in restoring my life. In the mighty and matchless name of Jesus, I pray, Amen.

Prayer 325: God's Goodness in Every Season

Scripture:

"Oh, taste and see that the Lord is good; blessed is the man who trusts in Him."

(Psalm 34:8 KJV)

Prayer:

Father, I thank You for Your goodness that is evident in my life. I want to experience the fullness of Your blessings and trust in Your faithful provision. Help me to see Your goodness in every circumstance.

Lord, when I feel discouraged, remind me of the countless ways You have shown Your love. Let my heart overflow with gratitude as I reflect on Your faithfulness.

Thank You, Lord, for Your goodness that never fades. In the mighty and matchless name of Jesus, I pray, Amen.

Prayer 326: God's Joy in My Heart

Scripture:

"The joy of the Lord is your strength."

(Nehemiah 8:10 KJV)

Prayer:

Father, I thank You for the joy that comes from knowing You. Your joy strengthens my heart and lifts my spirit. Help me to embrace that joy, even in difficult times.

Lord, when life's challenges threaten to overshadow my joy, remind me to focus on the blessings You have provided. Let Your joy fill my heart and overflow into my interactions with others.

Thank You, Lord, for the joy that sustains me. In the mighty and matchless name of Jesus, I pray, Amen.

Prayer 327: God's Assurance in Uncertainty

Scripture:

"The heart of man plans his way, but the Lord establishes his steps."
(Proverbs 16:9 ESV)

Prayer:

Father, I thank You for the assurance that You are in control of my life. While I may have my plans, I trust that You are establishing my steps. Help me to submit my desires to You and to seek Your guidance in every decision.

Lord, when I feel uncertain about the future, remind me that You are directing my path. Let me find peace in knowing that You are always working for my good.

Thank You, Lord, for establishing my steps. In the mighty and matchless name of Jesus, I pray, Amen.

Prayer 328: God's Faithfulness Through Every Trial

Scripture:

"For the Lord is good; His steadfast love endures forever, and His faithfulness to all generations."

(Psalm 100:5 ESV)

Prayer:

Father, I thank You for Your unwavering faithfulness. You are good, and Your love endures through every trial I face. Help me to remember Your past faithfulness as I navigate present challenges.

Lord, when I feel overwhelmed, remind me that Your love is steadfast. Let me lean on Your promises, trusting that You will see me through every difficulty.

Thank You, Lord, for being my faithful companion through all of life's challenges. In the mighty and matchless name of Jesus, I pray, Amen.

Prayer 329: God's Love in My Relationships

Scripture:

"Above all, keep loving one another earnestly, since love covers a multitude of sins."
(1 Peter 4:8 ESV)

Prayer:

Father, I thank You for the gift of love in my relationships. Help me to love others deeply and selflessly, just as You have loved me. Teach me to extend grace and forgiveness, allowing love to prevail in all my interactions.

Lord, when I encounter conflict or frustration, remind me of the power of love. Let me choose to respond with kindness and understanding, reflecting Your love to those around me.

Thank You, Lord, for the gift of love. In the mighty and matchless name of Jesus, I pray, Amen.

Prayer 330: God's Comfort in Times of Trouble

Scripture:

"God is our refuge and strength, a very present help in trouble."

(Psalm 46:1 KJV)

Prayer:

Father, I thank You for being my refuge and strength in times of trouble. I can always turn to You for help. Help me to remember that You are my safe place, where I can find comfort and security.

Lord, when challenges arise, remind me that You are with me. Let me find peace in knowing that You are guiding and supporting me through every storm.

Thank You, Lord, for being my ever-present help in times of trouble. In the mighty and matchless name of Jesus, I pray, Amen.

Prayer 331: God's Healing Touch

Scripture:

"And the prayer of faith will save the one who is sick, and the Lord will raise him up."

(James 5:15 ESV)

Prayer:

Father, I thank You for the healing that comes through faith in You. I trust in Your ability to heal both body and spirit. Help me to bring my needs before You with confidence, believing in Your power to restore.

Lord, when I or my loved ones face illness, remind me to seek You first. Let my prayers be filled with faith, knowing that You are the ultimate healer.

Thank You, Lord, for Your healing touch in my life. In the mighty and matchless name of Jesus, I pray, Amen.

Prayer 332: God's Assurance of His Goodness

Scripture:

"Oh, taste and see that the Lord is good; blessed is the man who trusts in Him."

(Psalm 34:8 KJV)

Prayer:

Father, I thank You for Your goodness that is evident in my life. I want to experience the fullness of Your blessings and trust in Your faithful provision. Help me to see Your goodness in every situation.

Lord, when I feel discouraged, remind me of the countless ways You have shown Your love. Let my heart overflow with gratitude as I reflect on Your faithfulness.

Thank You, Lord, for Your goodness that never fades. In the mighty and matchless name of Jesus, I pray, Amen.

Prayer 333: God's Strength in Every Challenge

Scripture:

"I can do all things through Christ who strengthens me."
(Philippians 4:13 KJV)

Prayer:

Father, I thank You for the strength You provide in every challenge. I can face any situation because You empower me. Help me to rely on Your strength and to trust in Your ability to carry me through.

Lord, when I feel weak or overwhelmed, remind me that I can do all things through You. Let me walk confidently, knowing that Your power is at work within me.

Thank You, Lord, for the strength that sustains me. In the mighty and matchless name of Jesus, I pray, Amen.

Prayer 334: God's Comfort in My Pain

Scripture:

"He heals the brokenhearted and binds up their wounds."
(Psalm 147:3 ESV)

Prayer:

Father, I thank You for Your healing presence in my life. You see my pain and brokenness, and I trust in Your ability to mend my heart. Help me to bring my wounds to You, knowing that You care for me deeply.

Lord, when I feel overwhelmed by grief or hurt, remind me of Your promise to heal. Let Your loving presence bring comfort and restoration to every area of my life.

Thank You, Lord, for Your compassionate healing. In the mighty and matchless name of Jesus, I pray, Amen.

Prayer 335: God's Guidance in Every Decision

Scripture:

"Trust in the Lord with all your heart, and do not lean on your own understanding. In all your ways acknowledge Him, and He will make straight your paths."

(Proverbs 3:5-6 ESV)

Prayer:

Father, I thank You for the guidance You provide in my life. I choose to trust in You with my whole heart, knowing that Your ways are higher than mine. Help me to seek Your wisdom in every decision I make.

Lord, when I feel uncertain or confused, remind me to lean on You rather than my own understanding. Let me walk in faith, trusting that You are directing my steps.

Thank You, Lord, for being my source of guidance. In the mighty and matchless name of Jesus, I pray, Amen.

Prayer 336: God's Peace in My Life

Scripture:

"And the peace of God, which surpasses all understanding, will guard your hearts and your minds in Christ Jesus."
(Philippians 4:7 ESV)

Prayer:

Father, I thank You for the peace that comes from knowing You. I invite Your peace into my heart and mind, trusting that it will guard me against anxiety and fear. Help me to hold onto Your peace in every situation.

Lord, when troubling thoughts arise, remind me to focus on You. Let Your calming presence fill my heart, allowing me to rest in Your assurance.

Thank You, Lord, for the peace that surpasses all understanding. In the mighty and matchless name of Jesus, I pray, Amen.

Prayer 337: God's Love is Unchanging

Scripture:

"For I am convinced that neither death nor life, neither angels nor demons, neither the present nor the future, nor any powers, neither height nor depth, nor anything else in all creation, will be able to separate us from the love of God that is in Christ Jesus our Lord."
(Romans 8:38-39 ESV)

Prayer:

Father, I thank You for the assurance that nothing can separate me from Your love. Your love is unchanging and everlasting, and I am grateful for that truth. Help me to fully embrace Your love and to share it with those around me.

Lord, when I feel unworthy or distant, remind me of the depth of Your love. Let me rest in the assurance that I am forever loved and accepted by You.

Thank You, Lord, for Your everlasting love. In the mighty and matchless name of Jesus, I pray, Amen.

Prayer 338: God's Restoration in My Life

Scripture:

"And I will restore to you the years that the locust has eaten."

(Joel 2:25 KJV)

Prayer:

Father, I thank You for Your promise of restoration. You are the God who heals and makes all things new. Help me to trust in Your ability to bring restoration to every area of my life.

Lord, when I reflect on my past losses, remind me that You are a God who redeems and renews. Let me walk forward with hope, anticipating the healing You will bring.

Thank You, Lord, for Your faithfulness in restoring my life. In the mighty and matchless name of Jesus, I pray, Amen.

Prayer 339: God's Joy in My Heart

Scripture:

"The joy of the Lord is your strength."
(Nehemiah 8:10 KJV)

Prayer:

Father, I thank You for the joy that comes from knowing You. Your joy strengthens my heart and lifts my spirit. Help me to embrace that joy, even in difficult times.

Lord, when life's challenges threaten to overshadow my joy, remind me to focus on the blessings You have provided. Let Your joy fill my heart and overflow into my interactions with others.

Thank You, Lord, for the joy that sustains me. In the mighty and matchless name of Jesus, I pray, Amen.

Prayer 340: God's Assurance in Every Trial

Scripture:

"Many are the afflictions of the righteous, but the Lord delivers him out of them all."

(Psalm 34:19 KJV)

Prayer:

Father, I thank You for Your faithfulness in every trial I face. I trust in Your promise to deliver me from my afflictions. Help me to remain steadfast in my faith, knowing that You are always at work for my good.

Lord, when I feel overwhelmed, remind me of Your past deliverances. Let my faith be strengthened as I look back on how You have always been there for me.

Thank You, Lord, for Your unwavering faithfulness through every challenge. In the mighty and matchless name of Jesus, I pray, Amen.

Prayer 341: God's Love in Every Situation

Scripture:

"But God, who is rich in mercy, because of His great love with which He loved us."
(Ephesians 2:4 NKJV)

Prayer:

Father, I thank You for Your great love and mercy. Your love is a constant source of strength and comfort in my life. Help me to recognize and embrace Your love in every situation I face.

Lord, when I encounter difficulties or feel overwhelmed, remind me of the depth of Your love for me. Let me find solace in knowing that Your love covers all my shortcomings and fears.

Thank You, Lord, for the richness of Your love that sustains me. In the mighty and matchless name of Jesus, I pray, Amen.

Prayer 342: God's Peace in Turbulent Times

Scripture:

"The Lord will fight for you, and you have only to be silent."
(Exodus 14:14 ESV)

Prayer:

Father, I thank You for the assurance that You fight for me. In turbulent times, I can find peace knowing that I don't have to carry the burden alone. Help me to rest in Your protection and to trust in Your plans.

Lord, when I feel overwhelmed by challenges, remind me to be still and know that You are God. Let me find comfort in Your presence and the knowledge that You are actively working for my good.

Thank You, Lord, for being my defender and my peace. In the mighty and matchless name of Jesus, I pray, Amen.

Prayer 343: God's Guidance on My Path

Scripture:

"Your word is a lamp to my feet and a light to my path."
(Psalm 119:105 ESV)

Prayer:

Father, I thank You for the guidance found in Your Word. Your truth illuminates my path and helps me make wise decisions. Help me to seek Your Word daily, allowing it to direct my steps.

Lord, when I feel lost or confused, remind me to turn to Your truth for direction. Let Your Word be the light that guides me through every decision I face.

Thank You, Lord, for the light of Your Word. In the mighty and matchless name of Jesus, I pray, Amen.

Prayer 344: God's Restoration in My Life

Scripture:

"He will wipe every tear from their eyes, and there will be no more death or mourning or crying or pain, for the old order of things has passed away."

(Revelation 21:4 ESV)

Prayer:

Father, I thank You for the promise of restoration and healing. I trust that You will bring an end to my pain and sorrow, transforming my heart and life. Help me to hold onto hope as I wait for the renewal You have promised.

Lord, when I feel overwhelmed by my circumstances, remind me that You are working to restore all things. Let me walk in faith, anticipating the healing and renewal You will bring.

Thank You, Lord, for Your faithfulness in restoring my life. In the mighty and matchless name of Jesus, I pray, Amen.

Prayer 345: God's Strength in Every Trial

Scripture:

"He gives power to the weak, and to those who have no might He increases strength."
(Isaiah 40:29 NKJV)

Prayer:

Father, I thank You for the strength You provide when I feel weak. In my struggles, I can find power in You. Help me to lean on Your strength and to trust in Your ability to carry me through every trial.

Lord, when I face challenges that seem insurmountable, remind me that I am not alone. Let me walk confidently, knowing that Your strength is made perfect in my weakness.

Thank You, Lord, for being my source of strength and support. In the mighty and matchless name of Jesus, I pray, Amen.

Prayer 346: God's Joy in My Heart

Scripture:

"I have told you this so that my joy may be in you and that your joy may be complete."

(John 15:11 NIV)

Prayer:

Father, I thank You for the joy that comes from knowing You. Your joy completes my heart and fills my spirit. Help me to live in that joy daily, sharing it with those around me.

Lord, when I feel burdened by life's challenges, remind me of the joy I have in You. Let me focus on Your goodness and the blessings in my life, allowing that joy to overflow into my interactions with others.

Thank You, Lord, for the joy that sustains me. In the mighty and matchless name of Jesus, I pray, Amen.

Prayer 347: God's Protection Over My Life

Scripture:

"The name of the Lord is a strong tower; the righteous man runs into it and is safe."

(Proverbs 18:10 ESV)

Prayer:

Father, I thank You for being my strong tower and refuge. In times of trouble, I can find safety in Your name. Help me to trust in Your protection and to run to You in every situation.

Lord, when I feel threatened or anxious, remind me that I am safe in Your care. Let me find comfort in the assurance that You are always watching over me.

Thank You, Lord, for Your protection that surrounds me. In the mighty and matchless name of Jesus, I pray, Amen.

Prayer 348: God's Assurance of His Presence

Scripture:

"And behold, I am with you always, to the end of the age."
(Matthew 28:20 ESV)

Prayer:

Father, I thank You for the assurance that You are always with me. In times of fear and uncertainty, I can find comfort in Your presence. Help me to recognize Your guidance as I navigate life's challenges.

Lord, when I feel lonely or abandoned, remind me of Your promise to never leave me. Let me find strength in knowing that I am never alone.

Thank You, Lord, for being my constant companion. In the mighty and matchless name of Jesus, I pray, Amen.

Prayer 349: God's Love in My Life

Scripture:

"For I know the plans I have for you, declares the Lord, plans to prosper you and not to harm you, plans to give you hope and a future."

(Jeremiah 29:11 KJV)

Prayer:

Father, I thank You for the plans You have for my life. I trust that Your intentions are good and filled with hope. Help me to seek Your will and to trust in Your timing, especially when I feel uncertain about the future.

Lord, when I encounter obstacles, remind me that You have a plan for my life. Let me walk in faith, knowing that You are guiding me toward a bright future.

Thank You, Lord, for the hope and future You have prepared for me. In the mighty and matchless name of Jesus, I pray, Amen.

Prayer 350: God's Goodness in My Life

Scripture:

"Give thanks to the Lord, for He is good; His love endures forever."

(Psalm 107:1 NIV)

Prayer:

Father, I thank You for Your goodness that is evident in my life. I want to experience the fullness of Your blessings and trust in Your faithful provision. Help me to see Your goodness in every circumstance.

Lord, when I feel discouraged, remind me of the countless ways You have shown Your love. Let my heart overflow with gratitude as I reflect on Your faithfulness.

Thank You, Lord, for Your goodness that never fades. In the mighty and matchless name of Jesus, I pray, Amen.

Prayer 351: God's Strength in My Trials

Scripture:

"The Lord is my strength and my shield; my heart trusts in Him, and He helps me. My heart leaps for joy, and with my song I praise Him."

(Psalm 28:7 NIV)

Prayer:

Father, I thank You for being my strength and my shield. In every trial I face, I trust in Your ability to help me. Help me to lean on You and find joy in Your support, knowing that You are always there to lift me up.

Lord, when I feel overwhelmed by challenges, remind me that I can rely on Your strength. Let my heart leap for joy as I remember Your goodness and faithfulness.

Thank You, Lord, for being my strength and my shield. In the mighty and matchless name of Jesus, I pray, Amen.

Prayer 352: God's Comfort in Sorrow

Scripture:

"Blessed are those who mourn, for they shall be comforted."
(Matthew 5:4 ESV)

Prayer:

Father, I thank You for the promise of comfort for those who mourn. You understand my pain, and I trust that You will bring healing to my heart. Help me to seek Your comfort during this time of sorrow, knowing that You are always present.

Lord, when grief feels overwhelming, remind me of Your love and compassion. Let me find solace in Your presence, allowing Your comfort to fill my heart and restore my spirit.

Thank You, Lord, for being my comforter in times of need. In the mighty and matchless name of Jesus, I pray, Amen.

Prayer 353: God's Wisdom in Every Decision

Scripture:

"If any of you lacks wisdom, let him ask of God, who gives to all liberally and without reproach, and it will be given to him."
(James 1:5 NKJV)

Prayer:

Father, I thank You for the wisdom that comes from You. I ask for Your guidance in every decision I make, trusting that You will provide the understanding I need. Help me to seek You first in all things.

Lord, when I feel uncertain or confused, remind me to turn to Your Word for clarity. Let Your wisdom illuminate my path, leading me toward what is best.

Thank You, Lord, for being my source of wisdom. In the mighty and matchless name of Jesus, I pray, Amen.

Prayer 354: God's Joy in My Heart

Scripture:

"The joy of the Lord is your strength."
(Nehemiah 8:10 KJV)

Prayer:

Father, I thank You for the joy that comes from knowing You. Your joy strengthens my heart and lifts my spirit. Help me to embrace that joy, even in difficult times.

Lord, when life's challenges threaten to overshadow my joy, remind me to focus on the blessings You have provided. Let Your joy fill my heart and overflow into my interactions with others.

Thank You, Lord, for the joy that sustains me. In the mighty and matchless name of Jesus, I pray, Amen.

Prayer 355: God's Protection Over My Life

Scripture:

"The name of the Lord is a strong tower; the righteous man runs into it and is safe."
(Proverbs 18:10 ESV)

Prayer:

Father, I thank You for being my strong tower and refuge. In times of trouble, I can find safety in Your name. Help me to trust in Your protection and to run to You in every situation.

Lord, when I feel threatened or anxious, remind me that I am safe in Your care. Let me find comfort in the assurance that You are always watching over me.

Thank You, Lord, for Your protection that surrounds me. In the mighty and matchless name of Jesus, I pray, Amen.

Prayer 356: God's Assurance of His Love

Scripture:

"For I am convinced that neither death nor life, neither angels nor demons, neither the present nor the future, nor any powers, neither height nor depth, nor anything else in all creation, will be able to separate us from the love of God that is in Christ Jesus our Lord."

(Romans 8:38-39 ESV)

Prayer:

Father, I thank You for the assurance that nothing can separate me from Your love. Your love is unchanging and everlasting, and I am grateful for that truth. Help me to fully embrace Your love and to share it with those around me.

Lord, when I feel unworthy or distant, remind me of the depth of Your love. Let me rest in the assurance that I am forever loved and accepted by You.

Thank You, Lord, for Your everlasting love. In the mighty and matchless name of Jesus, I pray, Amen.

Prayer 357: God's Faithfulness in Every Challenge

Scripture:

"The steadfast love of the Lord never ceases; His mercies never come to an end."

(Lamentations 3:22 NKJV)

Prayer:

Father, I thank You for Your steadfast love and mercy that endure forever. I am grateful for Your faithfulness that sustains me through every challenge. Help me to remember Your goodness when I face difficulties.

Lord, when I feel overwhelmed, remind me that You are always there to support me. Let me cling to the truth that You are working for my good in every situation.

Thank You, Lord, for Your unwavering faithfulness. In the mighty and matchless name of Jesus, I pray, Amen.

Prayer 358: God's Restoration in My Life

Scripture:

"He will restore the years that the locust has eaten."
(Joel 2:25 KJV)

Prayer:

Father, I thank You for Your promise of restoration. You are able to bring healing and renewal to my life. Help me to trust in Your ability to restore what has been lost.

Lord, when I look back at my past, remind me that You can redeem and renew all things. Let me walk forward with hope, anticipating the restoration You will bring.

Thank You, Lord, for Your faithfulness in restoring my life. In the mighty and matchless name of Jesus, I pray, Amen.

Prayer 359: God's Joy in My Life

Scripture:

"You make known to me the path of life; in Your presence there is fullness of joy; at Your right hand are pleasures forevermore."

(Psalm 16:11 ESV)

Prayer:

Father, I thank You for the joy that comes from being in Your presence. I desire to experience the fullness of joy that only You can provide. Help me to seek You daily, knowing that true joy is found in communion with You.

Lord, when I feel overwhelmed by life's challenges, remind me of the joy I have in You. Let me focus on Your goodness and the blessings in my life, allowing that joy to overflow into my interactions with others.

Thank You, Lord, for the joy that fills my heart. In the mighty and matchless name of Jesus, I pray, Amen.

Prayer 360: God's Assurance in Every Situation

Scripture:

"For I know the plans I have for you, declares the Lord, plans to prosper you and not to harm you, plans to give you hope and a future."

(Jeremiah 29:11 KJV)

Prayer:

Father, I thank You for the plans You have for my life. I trust that Your intentions are good and filled with hope. Help me to seek Your will and to trust in Your timing, especially when I feel uncertain about the future.

Lord, when I encounter obstacles, remind me that You are in control. Let me walk in faith, knowing that You are guiding me toward a bright future.

Thank You, Lord, for the hope and future You have prepared for me. In the mighty and matchless name of Jesus, I pray, Amen.

Prayer 361: God's Strength in My Weakness

Scripture:

"But He said to me, 'My grace is sufficient for you, for My power is made perfect in weakness.' Therefore I will boast all the more gladly about my weaknesses, so that Christ's power may rest on me."

(2 Corinthians 12:9 NKJV)

Prayer:

Father, I thank You for Your grace that is sufficient for all my needs. In my weaknesses, I find strength in You. Help me to embrace my limitations and rely on Your power to guide me through every challenge.

Lord, when I feel inadequate or overwhelmed, remind me that Your strength is made perfect in my weakness. Let me walk in confidence, knowing that I am empowered by Your grace.

Thank You, Lord, for Your sufficient grace in my life. In the mighty and matchless name of Jesus, I pray, Amen.

Prayer 362: God's Comfort in Times of Distress

Scripture:

"The Lord is near to the brokenhearted and saves the crushed in spirit."

(Psalm 34:18 ESV)

Prayer:

Father, I thank You for being near to me in times of distress. You understand my pain, and I trust that You will bring healing to my heart. Help me to seek Your comfort during difficult times, knowing that You are always present.

Lord, when I feel crushed by grief or sorrow, remind me that You are my refuge. Let Your love surround me, bringing peace and restoration to my spirit.

Thank You, Lord, for being my comforter in times of need. In the mighty and matchless name of Jesus, I pray, Amen.

Prayer 363: God's Assurance of His Guidance

Scripture:

"I will instruct you and teach you in the way you should go; I will counsel you with My eye upon you."

(Psalm 32:8 ESV)

Prayer:

Father, I thank You for the promise of Your guidance. You instruct and teach me, and I trust that You will lead me on the right path. Help me to be attentive to Your voice and to follow Your direction.

Lord, when I feel lost or uncertain, remind me to seek Your wisdom in prayer. Let Your counsel guide me through every decision I face.

Thank You, Lord, for being my constant guide. In the mighty and matchless name of Jesus, I pray, Amen.

Prayer 364: God's Peace in Every Storm

Scripture:

"He calms the storm, so that its waves are still."
                              (Psalm 107:29 NKJV)

Prayer:

Father, I thank You for the peace You bring even in the midst of the storm. I trust that You have the power to calm the chaos around me. Help me to seek Your presence when I feel overwhelmed by life's challenges.

Lord, when the storms of life threaten to disrupt my peace, remind me to turn to You for refuge. Let me find comfort in knowing that You are in control and that I am safe in Your care.

Thank You, Lord, for the peace that surpasses all understanding. In the mighty and matchless name of Jesus, I pray, Amen.

Prayer 365: God's Love Endures Forever

Scripture:

"Give thanks to the Lord, for He is good; His love endures forever."

(Psalm 136:1 KJV)

Prayer:

Father, I thank You for Your goodness and the enduring nature of Your love. Your love is a constant source of strength and comfort in my life. Help me to recognize and embrace Your love in every situation I encounter.

Lord, when I feel lost or alone, remind me that Your love never fails. Let me walk confidently in the knowledge that I am cherished and accepted by You.

Thank You, Lord, for Your everlasting love that sustains me. In the mighty and matchless name of Jesus, I pray, Amen.

Reader's Prayer

As I come before You today, I lift up every reader of this prayer book into Your loving hands. I pray that You cover them with Your grace, peace, and protection. May Your presence surround them, guiding their hearts and minds in all that they do.

Lord, I ask that You fill their lives with hope and joy, reminding them of Your unwavering love and faithfulness. Grant them the strength to face each day with courage and confidence, knowing that they are never alone.

May every prayer they have spoken be a fragrant offering to You, and may they experience Your answers in ways that affirm their faith. Help them to seek You daily, finding comfort in Your Word and assurance in Your promises.

In the mighty and matchless name of Jesus, I declare blessings over their lives—blessings of restoration, healing, and abundance. May they walk in Your truth and share Your love with others, becoming vessels of Your grace in this world.

Amen.

Final Word of Encouragement

Dear reader,

As you journey through life, remember that prayer is not just a practice; it is a lifeline that connects you to the heart of God. Embrace the power of prayer and allow it to transform your life. In every challenge, in every moment of joy, and in every season of waiting, let prayer be your first response.

You are deeply loved and cherished by your Creator. Trust in His plans for you, and never lose sight of the hope that lies ahead. God is faithful, and He is always at work in your life, even when you cannot see it.

Continue to seek Him earnestly, and you will find Him. Let your heart be open to His leading, and remember that with God, all things are possible.

Stay blessed, and may the light of Christ shine brightly in you and through you. With love and encouragement,

Apostle BJ Christmas

Made in the USA
Columbia, SC
10 December 2024

48987258R00212